# MARVIN D. CONE

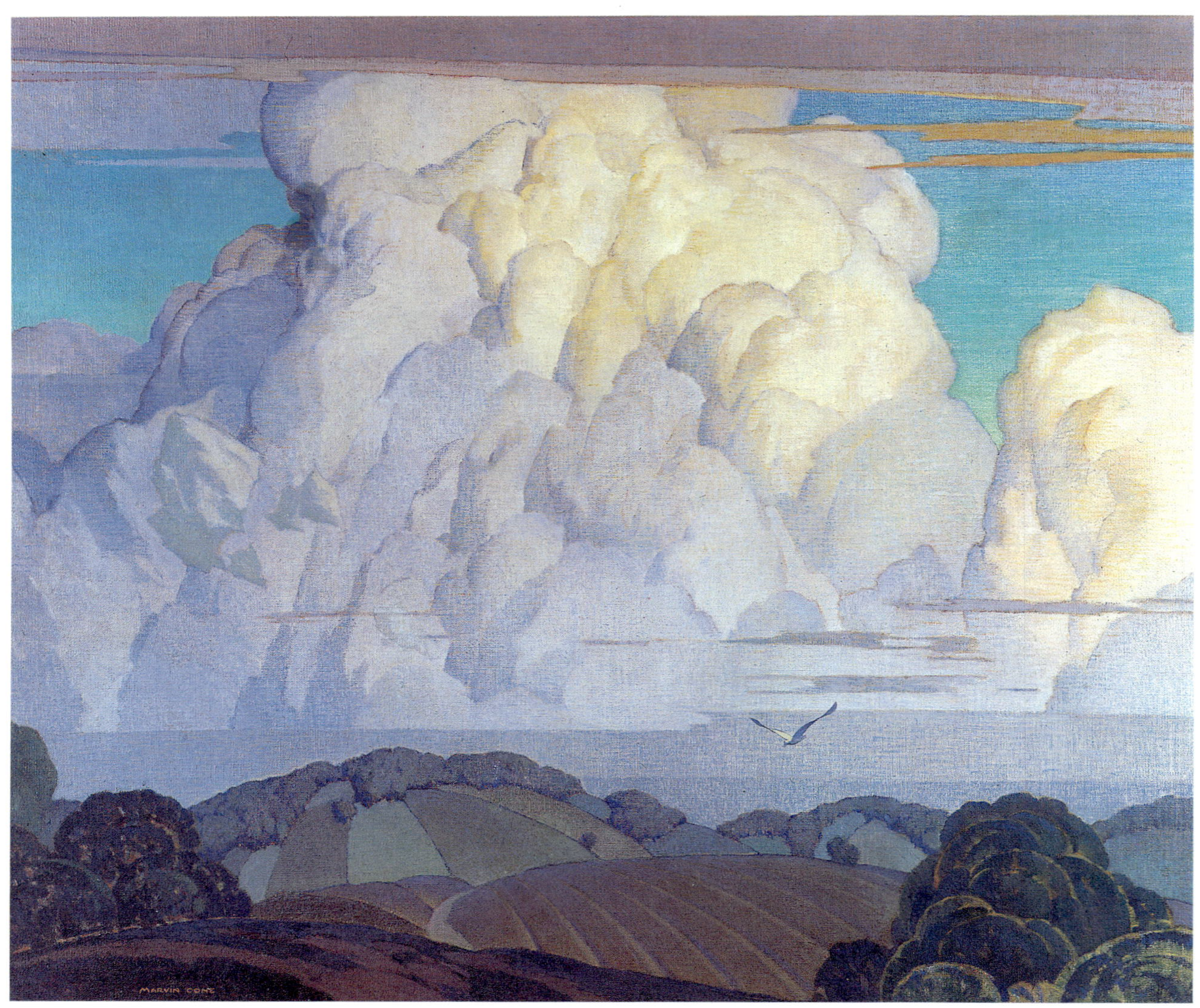


*Prelude,* 1931. Oil on canvas, 30½″ x 36″. (Cedar Rapids Museum of Art; Community School District Collection, 1970)

# MARVIN D. CONE

## An American Tradition

Joseph S. Czestochowski

Foreword by Paul Engle

E. P. DUTTON, INC.     NEW YORK

For Winnifred Cone, John B. Turner II,
and their friend J.-F. Stefan Parker

## ACKNOWLEDGMENTS

Many individuals participated in the completion of this project. I am particularly grateful to Winnifred Cone for her tremendous support, a loving testimony of her lifelong devotion to Marvin and his art. John B. Turner II deserves a special acknowledgment for his vision in establishing a permanent Marvin Cone collection at the Cedar Rapids Art Association. His friendship, enthusiasm, and constant encouragement will always be appreciated. It is a further tribute to Marvin Cone that his longtime friend and distinguished writer, Paul Engle, provided an exquisite foreword to this publication.

My thanks to Debra N. Czestochowski for her patience and her seasoned criticism, and to Stefan Parker who afforded me periodic respites. Cyril I. Nelson, my editor at E. P. Dutton, deserves particular thanks for his keen interest in Marvin Cone's art. Also, George Henry requires special mention for his splendid photography. At the Cedar Rapids Museum of Art, Marna Rehage, Monica Kindraka, Cindy Gewecke, and Reino Tuomala deserve thanks for their assistance. I should also like to acknowledge the Art Association Board of Trustees-Directors and the many friends of the Museum of Art for their continued and generous support.

Finally, I want to thank the many individuals and institutions who graciously agreed to share their collection with me: Doris and Reginald Weeks, Winnifred Cone, Bea Huston, Robert O. Daniel, Wendy and Peter Turner, Mr. and Mrs. Arthur A. Collins, Mr. and Mrs. Haven Y. Simmons, Coe College, Mrs. James Cooper, Cedar Rapids Area Chamber of Commerce, Cedar Rapids Community School District, Isobel Howell Brown, Mr. and Mrs. Robert Armstrong, Gordon Fennell, Mrs. Herbert S. Stamats, Mrs. Max Daehler, Irving L. and Kathryn H. Churchill, Peter O. Stamats, Mr. and Mrs. Fred C. Fisher, John S. Vavra, Iowa Electric Light & Power Company, Keith DeBolt, Mr. and Mrs. D. William Coppock, Mr. and Mrs. John Bickel, Sr., Mr. and Mrs. William P. Whipple, and Thomas B. Powell, Jr.

*First published, 1985, in the United States by E. P. Dutton, Inc., New York.*  *For information contact: E. P. Dutton, Inc., 2 Park Avenue, New York, N.Y. 10016. Library of Congress Catalog Card Number: 84-71978. Printed and bound by Dai Nippon Printing Co., Ltd., Tokyo, Japan. ISBN: 0-525-24300-3 (cloth) 0-525-48149-4 (DP). Published simultaneously in Canada by Fitzhenry & Whiteside Limited, Toronto*
*W 10 9 8 7 6 5 4 3 2 1 First Edition*

# CONTENTS

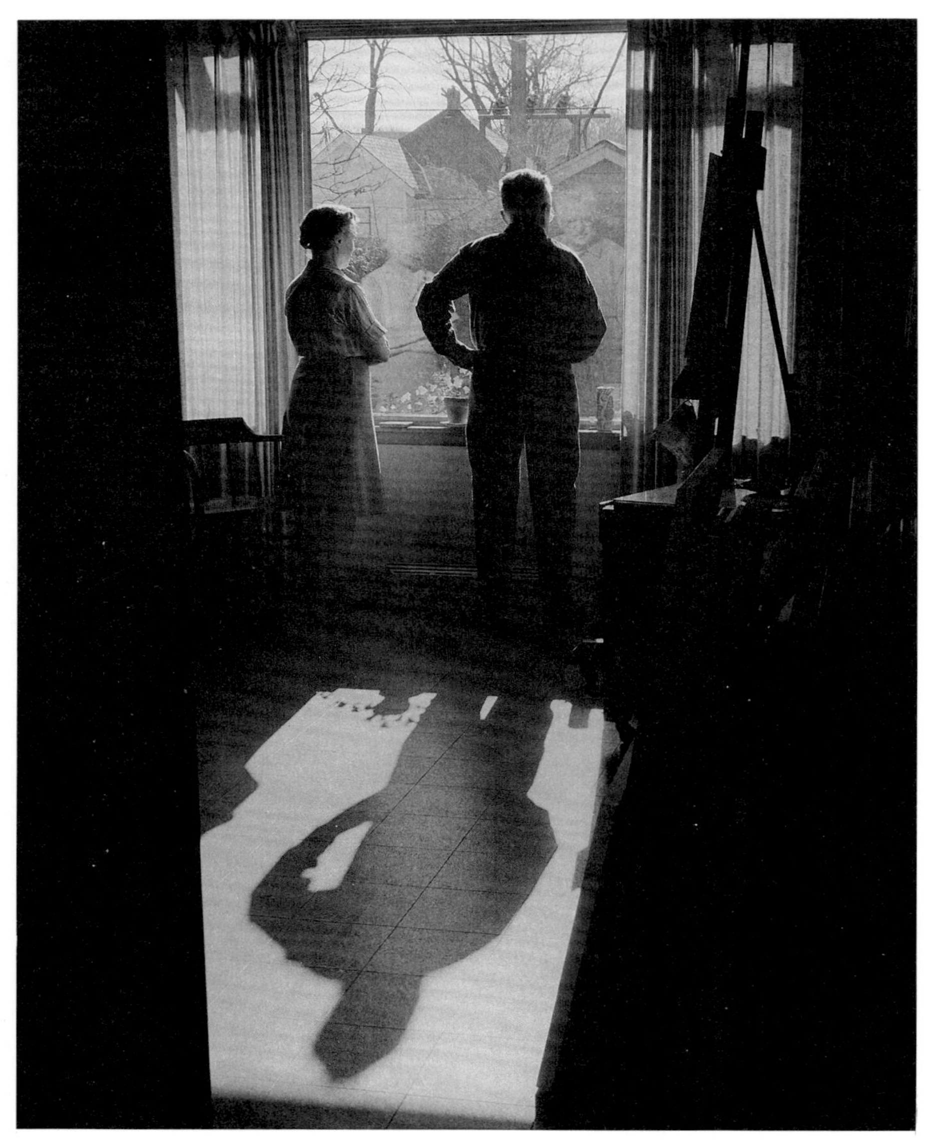

*Reflections: Portrait of Winnifred and Marvin, 1962.* Photograph courtesy George T. Henry.

# FOREWORD

Marvin was as good an artist as he was a man.
This is the highest praise, for he was a wonderful man.
Beautiful art is not made by ugly people.
He had a harmony in his life as he did in his painting.

For years he picked up at her apartment an older faculty lady at Coe who had a crippled leg. He drove her to the college and drove her home in the afternoon. Few people were aware. As he was naturally talented, he was also naturally kind. His acts of generosity were as instinctive as those subtle images that flowed into his imagination before they ran down his arm and brush onto the lucky canvas.

The Cones, Marvin, Winnifred, and Doris, lived in the next block to the Engles on Fifth Avenue SE in Cedar Rapids, Iowa, so that we saw each other often. We would go to them for dinner. Winnifred would push into a corner the wheeled tea cart on which Marvin kept his brushes and paints. He probably had the smallest painting space, about four feet square, of any artist ever. No complaints.

Summers my then wife, Mary Nissen, and I lived in the great house at Stone City called The Mansion, where Grant Wood had his art colony, a great, failed idea. The Cones would come out for a couple of weeks. We had a wood-burning range called a Smoke Eater, which required lots of fuel. Each morning I went out to chop wood. Winnifred would say, "Marvin, Paul is chopping. Go help." And each morning Marvin would reply, "Winnifred, I'm not only no good with an ax, I'm dangerous."

All his life in art Marvin steadily grew. His paintings became more original, exploratory, subtle. Those fascinating door paintings were inspired by an old, decaying quarryworker's house on the farm at Stone City. He saw the slanting light on the slanting doors as the frame rotted. Always new shapes, new shifts of line and color, new subjects. It is a shame he never painted more portraits, for he was very good. He was a superb draftsman, as is shown in his face of his daughter and in a drawing we have of a stone basket of fruit that once sat on the front steps at Stone City.

From his early clouds to his late near-abstractions, Marvin pursued one goal: the essential form behind the external shape, the ideal idea behind the grit of reality. He never compromised, never cared about being fashionable, never pursued that death trap of artists: the commercial art gallery. He was content to receive fees for his work that were so small they were almost insulting. His income was as limited as his art was limitless. One day he said, "I'm getting a new car. It takes me so long to make payments on a car, by the time the last one is made, it's worn out." He made payments all his life.

He was modest beyond any artist I have known. He never envied the success and publicity of his old friend Grant Wood. He was devoted to two things: his family and his painting. I hope art-friendly Cedar Rapids will always be devoted to him.

PAUL ENGLE

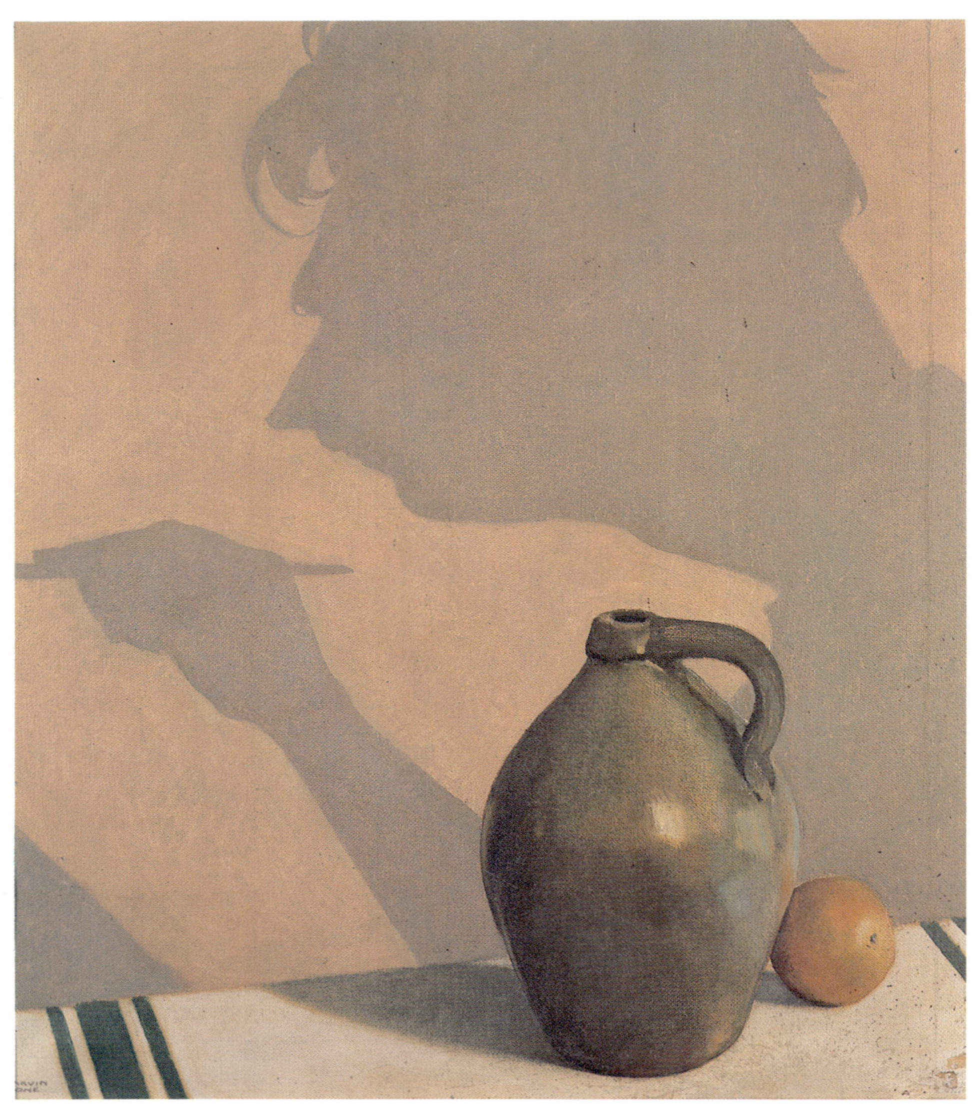

*Myself,* 1932–1933. Oil on canvas, 27″ x 24¼″. (Collection of Winnifred Cone)

# INTRODUCTION

American art of the 1930s is currently experiencing a resurgence of attention from collectors, museums, and the general public. One result of this renewed interest is the reassessment of many fine painters whose reputations have previously been overshadowed by those of such better known contemporaries as Grant Wood or Thomas Hart Benton. Marvin D. Cone (1891–1965) is one such artist whose achievements are noteworthy.

Marvin Cone—in contrast to his close friend Grant Wood—did not fit the popular conception of an artist, neither did he share a sense of mission about regionalism. His life was relatively unremarkable. He lived all of his seventy-four years in Cedar Rapids, Iowa, where he married, raised a family, and taught art classes for over forty years. He was highly respected by his contemporaries, but he never achieved great fame in the art world. Yet as conventional as his life may seem, his work shows him to have been a passionate artist who possessed a rare sensitivity to his environment. It is clear from this survey that Cone was an exquisite craftsman and an important artist in the long tradition of American landscape painting.

Cone's paintings may be roughly divided into four periods. The years from 1914 to 1929 were formative—a period when Cone first developed the stylistic tendencies that would continue through his mature work. Between 1930 and 1937, Cone concentrated on the landscape of the Midwest, capturing the special nuances of midwestern light and the complex formations of land and sky. These scenes, which rarely include people, are reminiscent of the Iowa countryside but without topographic precision. To the artist, the landscape had a poignant reality that was nonetheless unpredictable and elusive. Nature's sublimity, greater than its mere physical qualities, was Cone's principal pursuit.

The artist's interest in nature continued

throughout the 1940s, but at this time he also began to incorporate into his paintings such motifs as doors, windows, and hallways. These provided greater opportunities for technical virtuosity, and Cone created a number of haunting interiors with doors or windows revealing expansive voids beyond. The interiors, together with the group of animated carnival scenes done during the same period, frequently include a peering self-portrait and attest to the increasingly personal quality of Cone's work.

Finally, in the 1950s and 1960s, Cone created a powerful series of expressionistic interpretations of nature. Here Cone communicated in purely painterly terms his innermost feelings.

Cone's reason for painting did not parallel these stylistic changes. Although the artist did not leave extensive autobiographical comments, a few written statements offer considerable insight into his singular artistic purpose. On one occasion in 1947 he stated, "A work of art is a moving communication from an artist to a spectator. Therefore, when you look at a painting, don't worry too much about what it represents but look rather for the nature of the man who painted it—his spirit and fire."[1] It seems likely that Cone's lifelong objective was to increase his capacity for perception; to understand better and to reveal his surroundings and his own being. Also, each work reflects an individual moment of time and space, fixing Cone's identity within a universal context of inevitable change.

In retrospect, Cone was an important participant in America's long tradition of pantheism—a tradition that in literature includes Thoreau, Whitman, Burroughs, and Frost, to name a few; and in art, Cole, Inness, Homer, Burchfield, and O'Keeffe. Equally important, Cone was a community activist and a self-effacing teacher in the great tradition of Thomas P. Anshutz. Ultimately, although Cone's paintings open new vistas in our exploration of American art and display technical considerations achieved by few of his contemporaries, the artist would probably consider his devotion to his family, his friends, and community to be the most enduring achievement of his life.

## BEGINNINGS: EMERGING INTERESTS

Marvin Cone was born and raised in Cedar Rapids, where in 1906 he established a lifelong friendship with Grant Wood. Cone was graduated from Coe College in 1914 and also studied for several years at The Art Institute of Chicago School. His program of study there was diversified; class records at The Art Institute indicate that he excelled in drawing, and extant works show a strong design orientation. World War I interrupted his studies, and after being stationed in New Mexico, Cone left for France in 1917, where he served for several years as an interpreter. In 1919, Cone studied for three months at the School of Fine Arts in Montpellier, France, returning to Cedar Rapids to pursue his art interest. Commercial art was an available option, but at the time he chose to accept a position teaching French at Coe College for the 1919/20 academic year.

In Cedar Rapids, Cone quickly renewed both his friendship with Grant Wood and his active involvement with the local art association. Cone and

Wood went abroad in the summer of 1920, hoping to improve their technical skills. The visit proved influential, resulting in a stunning series of impressionistic views of picturesque cityscapes and landscapes: Paris streets and gardens, the French countryside. On the voyage home, an exhibition of thirty paintings was held in the ship's salon. The exhibit was quite popular, with his cloud paintings earning the most praise from critics. These Parisian works were the first to achieve success, and the decision to show them indicated his high regard for the results of the summer experience. Also, it was at the time of this exhibit that Grant introduced Marvin to Winnifred Swift, the future Mrs. Cone.

Cone returned to Cedar Rapids with a fresh perspective and immediately assumed expanded teaching duties at Coe College. In contrast to many of his contemporaries, who turned to teaching only as a last resort, Cone pursued it with an enthusiasm that continued for over forty years. He always maintained an extensive teaching schedule, including studio and art-history courses, and he benefited greatly from the daily exchange with students. Cone's commitment to his students was surpassed only by his devotion to his family. On one occasion in January 1927, he stated, "Without putting painting aside, my chief hobby is my four-year-old daughter, Doris, and what time I get to paint is most graciously awarded to me by her."[2]

The experience of a final trip to Europe, together with the emerging spirit of cultural nationalism, resolved Cone's need for a sense of place and further reinforced his confidence as an experienced craftsman. Financed by twenty community patrons, the Cones spent the summer of 1929 in Paris where he noted, "There is much to write about in Paris—much material of the guide book variety . . . but it seems to me that personal observation on the life in and around Paris might be more readable than the date of the completion of the metal roof on Chartres Cathedral, for instance."[3] Other letters home indicated how captivated he was by the luminosity of Paris, and the experience always held a key place in the pattern of his artistic growth.

Grant Wood subsequently observed of Cone, "Still keeping his strong use of pattern and design, this past season of working so long and so directly from nature has given a certain depth and connection to his work. Happily, this added realism has in no way diminished the poetry that has always been so characteristic of Marvin Cone's painting."[4] This painterly interest in the commonplace realities of the Parisian cityscape would soon be applied to his homeland. An active regional literature was also very influential, especially such writings by Ruth Suckow as *Country People* (1924) and *Iowa Interiors* (1926). This fascination was similarly popularized by the well-known American regionalists Thomas Hart Benton, John Steuart Curry, and Grant Wood. However, in contrast to these artists, Cone did not seek to create a documentary of nationalistic ambitions, but to articulate his vision of his being and surroundings. For Cone, painting was a private pursuit.

Increasingly, Cone preferred to work with a more sophisticated technique, including a stylized method of rendering forms—such as breaking down landscapes into layers of component parts—and using color rich with light. This tendency was seen in his 1919 painting of *Cloud Bank* (see p. 10). Many of these techniques predated by ten years similar developments in Wood's work; yet Cone avoided his friend's almost exclusive concern with design and the accompanying creation of an overly idealized environment.

A remarkable achievement of the 1920s was his *River Farm* (see p. 14), a striking composition and a turning point in this transition. This was one of the first paintings in which Cone pursued a systematic direction away from an Impressionistic aesthetic. A powerful affinity to a sense of place exists in this work, and Cone subtly shares his geographic and emotional commitment with us. The impact of the painting is conveyed by the interpretative design, and its meaning is derived from the slow contemplation of an isolated moment of time in space. Thus, during the 1920s, Cone consolidated his aesthetic vision and refined his technical abilities, becoming a product of his own "nativeness." As we shall discover, Cone emerged in the 1930s as a modern painter who approached a timeless landscape in a new and universal spirit.

## THE REGIONAL LANDSCAPE

The 1920s and 1930s were a period of profound transition and crisis in this country. Precipitated by the disillusionment of World War I and the shattering of Wilsonian idealism, a revival of isolationism swept the country. Individuals looked to the past with the earnest hope of understanding and rationalizing the present. Significant results were new popularity for the works of Mark Twain, Walt Whitman, contemporary regional writers, and the collecting of American folk art. In addition, the widely read Thomas Craven established the framework for a native art that was realistic in style and traditional in subject matter. These writings reflect the belief that art and culture function best when they deal with our native heritage and emphasize the traditional values that exemplify past achievements. What emerged from all this was an intensive search for cultural roots and an emphasis not on cities, skylines, or theories of form but on people and the landscape.

To many artists of the 1930s, including Cone, this prevailing mood prompted a retreat to certain values that had prospered between the 1820s and the 1850s, such as an interest in primeval or elemental nature and personal isolation or anonymity. Throughout these years, the message was clear: The progress of the American people and their culture was directly associated with the environment. Nature was not only a symbol of national vitality but also a source of virtue, a place to contemplate the sublime and an avenue for spiritual sustenance. As a consequence, we can find in the work of Cone—as well as that of John Marin, Edward Hopper, Marsden Hartley, Charles Burchfield, and others—various qualities that had inspired the landscapists of the nineteenth century. These artists turned to their local environment in pursuit of sources for their art. At the same time, such realist modes of painting were actively competing with a rising surge of stylistic alternatives.

It is from a similar context that Cone's art developed.

Cone's paintings of the 1930s epitomize his work. For example, in the stunning 1931 painting, *Prelude* (see p. ii), the colors are subtle and evocative in their suggestion of light, and the rolling hills, the fields and trees in the landscape, as well as the clouds in the huge lateral expanse of sky are given a sense of depth through a complex layering of forms. While the painting is a powerful statement of the mysteries of nature, it is also extremely personal in its sense of solitude and tranquillity. This quality was prevalent in the work of his contemporaries and had inspired much of the nineteenth-century landscape painting; yet Cone's painting of *Prelude* and other paintings of the 1930s were clearly modern and achieved a fresh perspective.

As such, it is curious to note a passage in Alexis de Tocqueville's 1831 *Journey to America* that seems poignantly to foreshadow Cone's painting.

> Who will ever paint a true picture of those rare moments in life when physical well-being prepares the way for calm of soul, and the universe seems before your eyes to have reached a perfect equilibrium; then the soul, half asleep, hovers between the present and the future, between the real and the possible, while with natural beauty all around and the air tranquil and mild, at peace with himself in the midst of universal peace, man listens to the even beating of his arteries that seems to him to mark the passage of time flowing drop by drop through eternity.[5]

If in *Prelude* and other works of the 1930s Cone shared with fellow regionalists a search for cultural roots, he also saw his landscapes as optimistic symbols for a revitalized nation.

In the summers of 1932 and 1933, Marvin Cone was, with his friend Grant Wood, an active force in the Stone City Art Colony. The objective of the colony was summarized as follows: "It is our belief that a true art expression must grow up from the environment itself. Then an American art will arrive through the fusion of various regional expressions based on a thorough analysis of what is significant to these regions."[6] The writer went on to state that it was not the colony's aim to create an American style or to impose a distinctive technique on others. The objective was, instead, to allow the participant to arrive at a personal vision that expressed the nuances of his specific surroundings. Unfortunately, the financial effect of the Depression closed the colony after only two summers. Subsequently, Wood assumed a faculty position at the University of Iowa, while Cone was appointed a professor of painting at Coe College. Through the 1930s, the Stone City area continued to provide the setting for many of Cone's best paintings, because the family would invariably summer there with the Paul Engles.

## NEW DIRECTIONS

During 1938/39, Cone secured a leave of absence from his teaching duties at Coe College. Cone termed it "a year of freedom," and the opportunity proved a tremendous catalyst to his painting. An isolated downtown studio was secured, and Cone set about his task in typical fashion, arriving at 9:00 A.M. each day, dressed in a coat and tie. He thrived, creating one distinguished work after another and also actively participated in numerous national invitational and competitive exhibitions. At the same time, his subject matter became more diversified, including not only his characteristic landscapes but also haunting interiors with ghosts and doors and circus and carnival scenes with a wealth of character study. Cone preferred this solitude and as such, it is not surprising that he would become fascinated with the abstract qualities of interior spaces. This desire to change his subject matter suggests that Cone was not guided by a philosophy of cultural isolationism; unlike Benton, Curry, and Wood, he recognized the limitations of dealing with an isolated segment in lieu of more universal subjects.

After working eight hours at his painting, Cone's favorite relaxation was reading mystery and detective stories at home. It is no surprise that he became interested in ghosts and that he considered *Anniversary* (see p. 34) to be among his best works of 1938. Painted with only black, white, yellow, and the resulting blends of greens, this work posed a considerable technical and compositional challenge. A sense of calm prevails over this and similar scenes because all potentially disturbing color contrasts have been eliminated. However, Cone's satisfaction was in realizing that he had not only created a pleasing painting but had also solved a difficult design problem.

In 1939, a rare glimpse of Cone's personal views was provided when he stated,

> The purpose of art is not to reproduce life, but to present an editorial, a comment on life. . . . The artist does not set out to imitate nature. What would be the purpose of that? Let the camera with its clever mechanism imitate. Art, such as poetry, music, and painting, is simply a portion of the experience of the artist. When we actually see ideals, they become real to us. Art traces an abstraction and makes it audible or visual. It symbolizes the whole of life. We believe in something we can see.[7]

Increasingly, in such works from 1939 as *Habitation* (see p. 41) and *Night Prowler* (see p. 42), Cone's pictures became more introspective and evocative of his inner feelings, like those of his contemporaries Edward Hopper, Milton Avery, Georgia O'Keeffe, and others. Cone's stunning achievement of 1931, *Prelude,* anticipated this change; at the same time, the "American Art Today" exhibition at the 1939 New York World's Fair confirmed it. Realism rather than modernism remained the dominant popular artistic style, but it was becoming more interpretative and psychological. For many artists, nature was becoming more a source of forms, color, and spatial relationships than a source for realist painting. In 1946, the change was reflected in Cone's suggestive abstractions of muted color and simplified forms. These works are a powerful statement of the artist's inner feelings and the mystery of life. A visionary quality and unresolved tension exist in these works that heighten our awareness of an unseen reality. The only vestige of any human drama is the frequent portrait on the wall; so that the viewer immediately becomes lost in the dream and contemplates the emptiness. For Cone, these scenes were perhaps nostalgic encounters with his memories, but they were most certainly eternalized visions safe from the changes of time. Aesthetically, these scenes were Cone's bridge between realism and abstraction. It is curious that the strange haunting openness seen in room paintings such as *Dear Departed* (1946; see p. 53) was a quality that, in the 1950s, European critics would associate with the Abstract Expressionist movement and compare to the awesome physical size of this country.

## EXPRESSIONISTIC EXPLORATIONS

Marvin Cone continued to pursue his inner vision in the 1950s, attempting, in the words of William Cullen Bryant, "A sincere communication of his own moral and intellectual being."[8] Cone's self-absorption with nature and his awareness of contemporary stylistic trends inevitably brought him to a nonrealist aesthetic. The transition was a logical continuation of his early exploration and was not unexpected. Cone enthusiastically embraced the changes in American art during the 1950s, viewing them as an opportunity to communicate his spirit effectively while being challenged from a design standpoint. His luminous paintings, such as *Inner Light* (1950; see p. 58), were clearly psychological and cosmological.

At the same time *Rakish Steps* (1961; see p. 66) and *Enigma* (1961; see p. 67) revealed a new style of painting that was championed by the Abstract Expressionists. Although their work was stylistically distinct, these artists did not represent a break in tradition. They did not turn their back on American painting between the world wars or on nineteenth-century landscape painting. In fact, critics have noted that even after Hiroshima the worship of primeval nature had reached mythic extremes: it was as if, following the apocalypse, artists needed to experience the first days of creation. A contemporary, Arshile Gorky, defined *abstraction* in terms that were clearly shared by Cone:

> Abstraction is the key factor of the creative imagination . . . and . . . enables man to break the finite barrier and enter into infinity. . . . It is the probing vehicle, the progressive thrust toward higher civilization. Mere realistic art is, therefore, finite and limits man only to the perception of his physical eyes. Namely, that which is tangible. Abstract art enables the artist to perceive beyond the tangible, to extract the infinite out of the finite. It is the emancipator of the mind. It is an exploration into unknown areas.[9]

Throughout these years Cone's moods grew to be more generalized, displaying a singular absorption in the future, probing the secrets of life, nature, and the world of the spirit. A gentle aura permeates Cone's works between 1950 and 1965. This does not imply that there is any faltering in his technical skills, indeed, some of his most powerfully evocative paintings were done during this time. It seems as if Cone was aware that he had arrived at his preferred style, knew what he wanted to express, and was content with his human transience. Ultimately, it is evident that many of these works were not only visual representations of Cone's lifelong quest for a definition of nature but also its relationship to his own being.

## CONCLUSION

Cone's work was well known to his contemporaries through his association with Wood, his extensive participation in national competitions, and his key involvement in founding and running the Stone City Art Colony in Iowa, which brought together a group of regionalist painters in the summers of 1932 and 1933. But unlike many of the artists associated with regionalist and American Scene painting of the 1930s, Cone did not seek to create a documentary or realistic depiction of the rural landscape but rather to evoke his inner vision of nature. To Cone, nature acted as a vehicle for revealing certain truths. His paintings were conceived by a complex process that integrated firsthand observation of nature with the artist's memories and feelings about what he had seen: a creative synthesis of the classic imagery of landscape painting with meaning that transcends simple representation. The poet Paul Engle wrote about this quality of Cone, "He stares at the world with his hands. . . . He has the painter's second sight, the form seen once, and then again, after the imagination has redefined it."[10]

## NOTES

1. Information from the files of Winnifred Cone, manuscript dated 1947.

2. Quoted in Robert Cron, "Marvin Cone—A True Artist," *Cedar Rapids Republican,* 30 January 1927, p. 2.

3. Quoted in "Marvin Cone Describes Life in Paris as Artist Sees It," *Cedar Rapids Gazette,* 18 August 1929, p. 3.

4. Quoted in "Art News of the Little Gallery," *Cedar Rapids Gazette,* 6 December 1929, p. 27.

5. Alexis de Tocqueville, *Journey to America* (1831) (Garden City, N.Y.: Doubleday Anchor, 1971), p. 398.

6. Quoted in Grant Wood, "Aim of the Colony," *Stone City Colony and Art School* (Summer 1933), brochure.

7. Quoted in *Cedar Rapids Gazette,* 19 January 1938, p. 15, and 26 May 1938, p. 8.

8. John W. McCoubrey, *American Art 1700–1960, Sources and Documents* (Englewood Cliffs, N.J.: Prentice-Hall, 1965), p. 96.

9. Arshile Gorky, letter, 17 February 1947; quoted in Kynaston McShine et al., *The Natural Paradise. Painting in America 1800–1950* (New York: The Museum of Modern Art, 1976), pp. 125–127.

10. Paul Engle, "Portrait of the Artist as Neighbor," *Marvin Cone, A Retrospective Exhibition 1938–1960* (Iowa City, Iowa: University of Iowa Department of Art, 1960), unpaged.

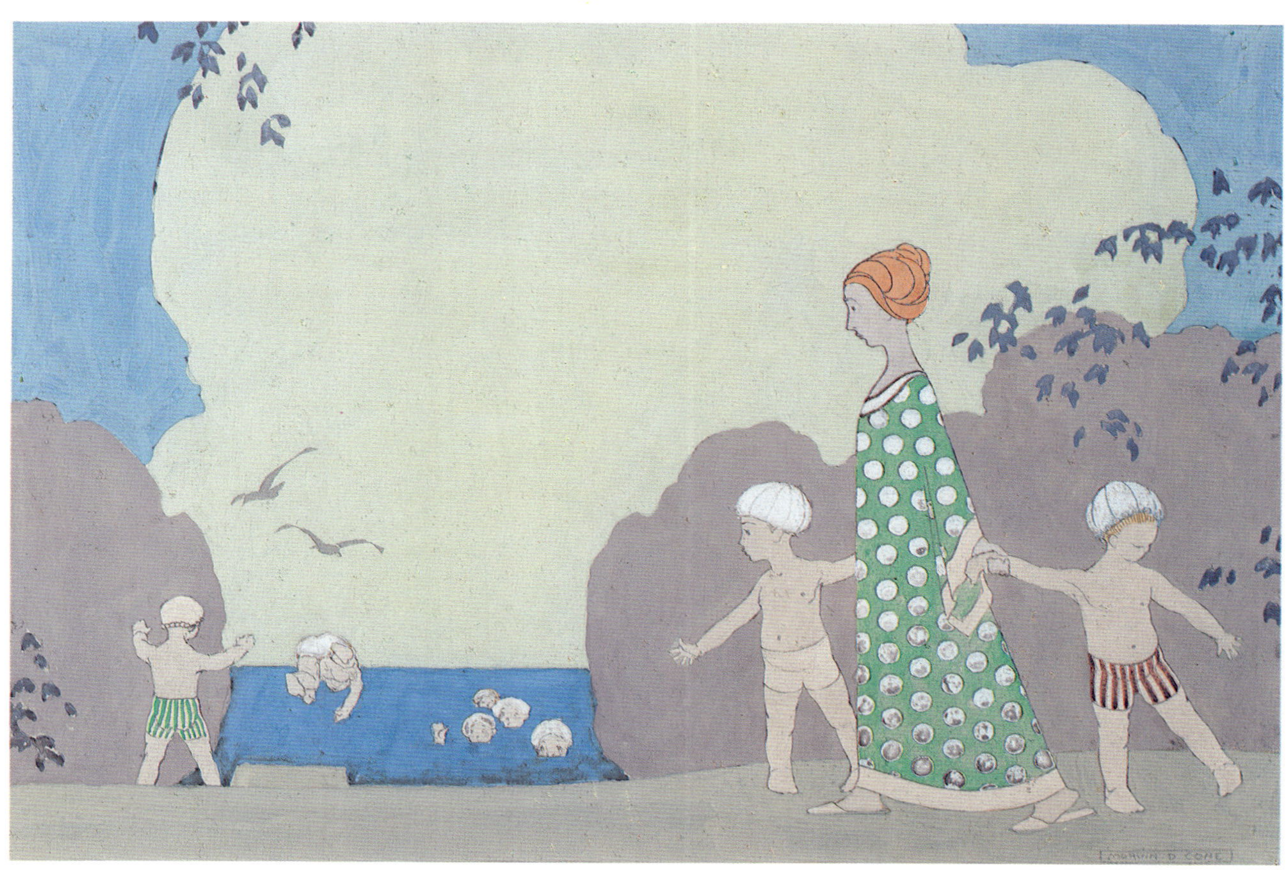

*At the Beach*, c. 1915. Gouache and pencil on paper, 8″ x 12″. (Cedar Rapids Museum of Art; Gift of Winnifred Cone and Family, and Museum Purchase, 1983)

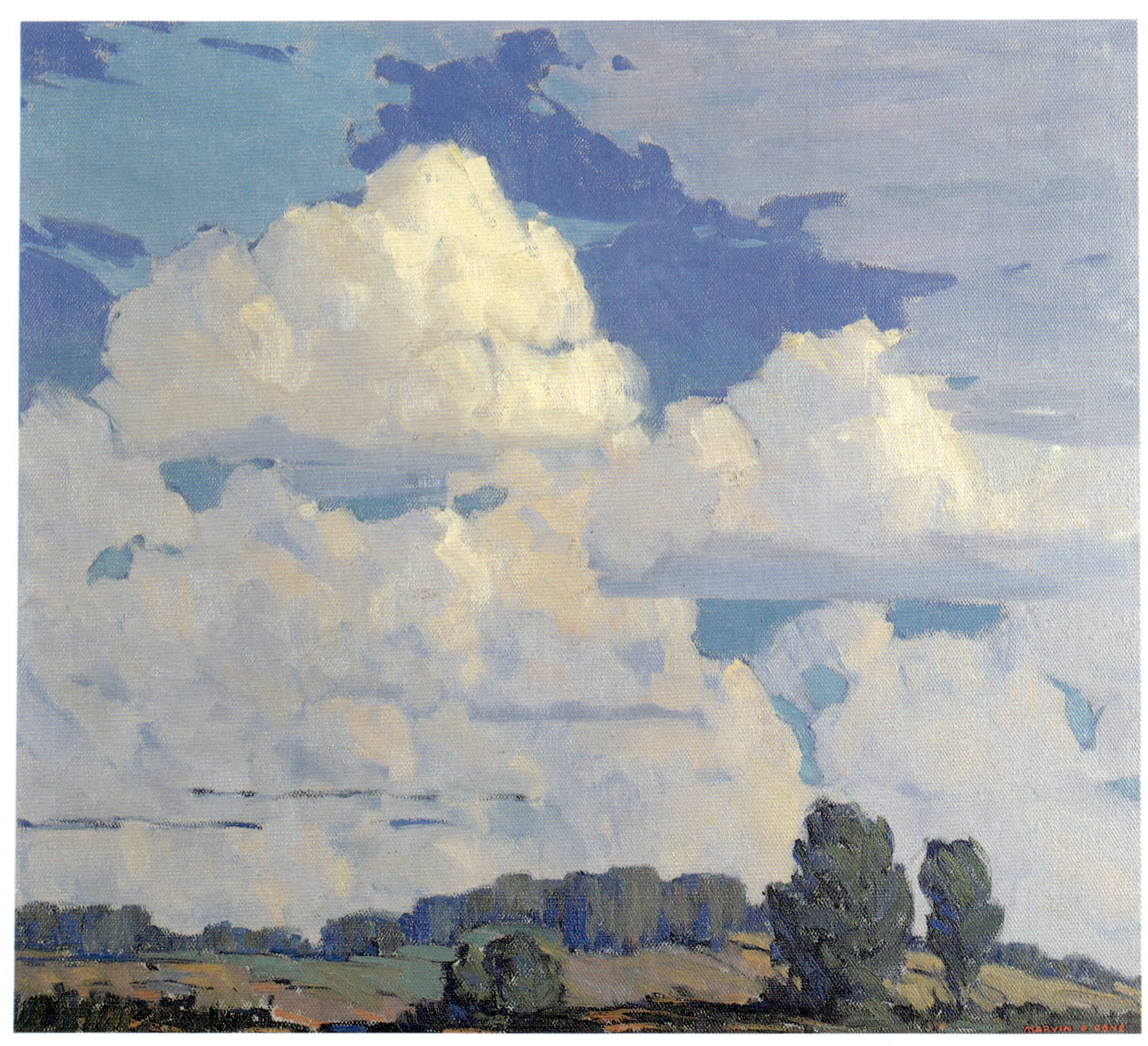

*Cloud Bank*, 1919. Oil on canvas, 18″ x 20″. (Cedar Rapids Museum of Art; Art Association Purchase, 1932)

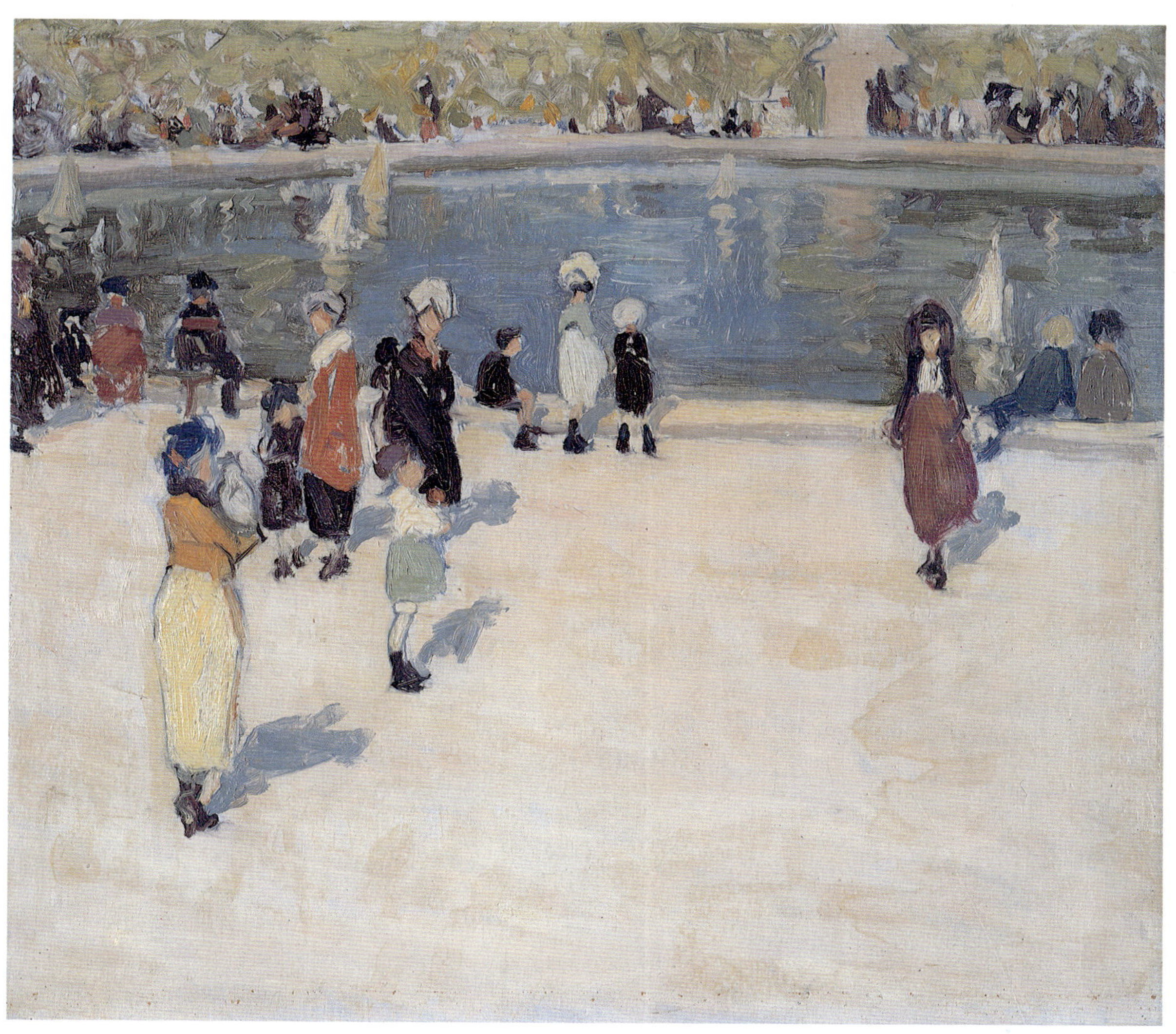

*Luxembourg Gardens,* 1920. Oil on panel, 13″ x 15″. (Collection of Mr. and Mrs. Arthur A. Collins)

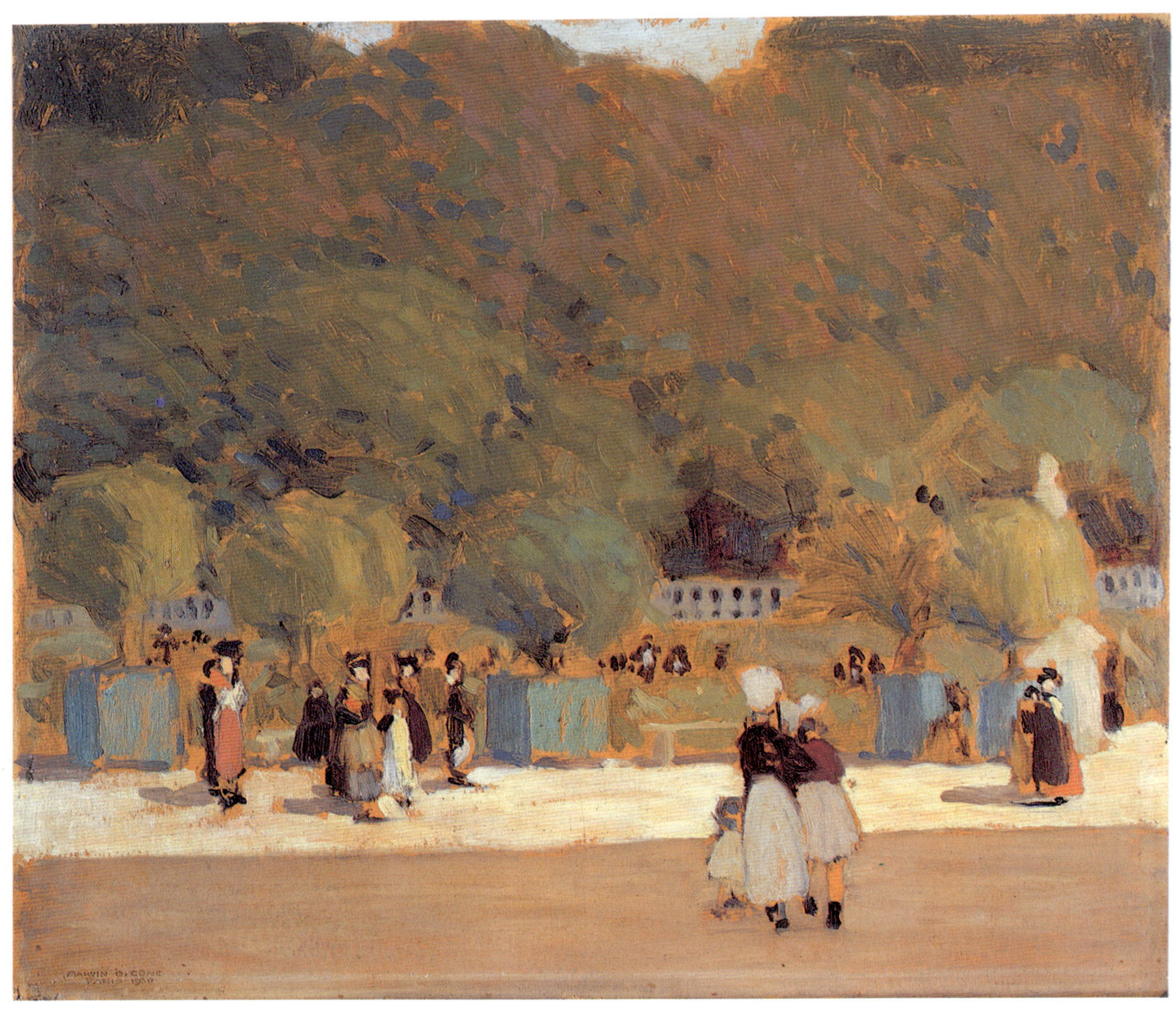

*A Bit of Sun—Luxembourg Gardens,* 1920. Oil on composition board, 13″ x 15″
(Cedar Rapids Museum of Art; Gift of Mr. and Mrs. Haven Y. Simmons, 1982)

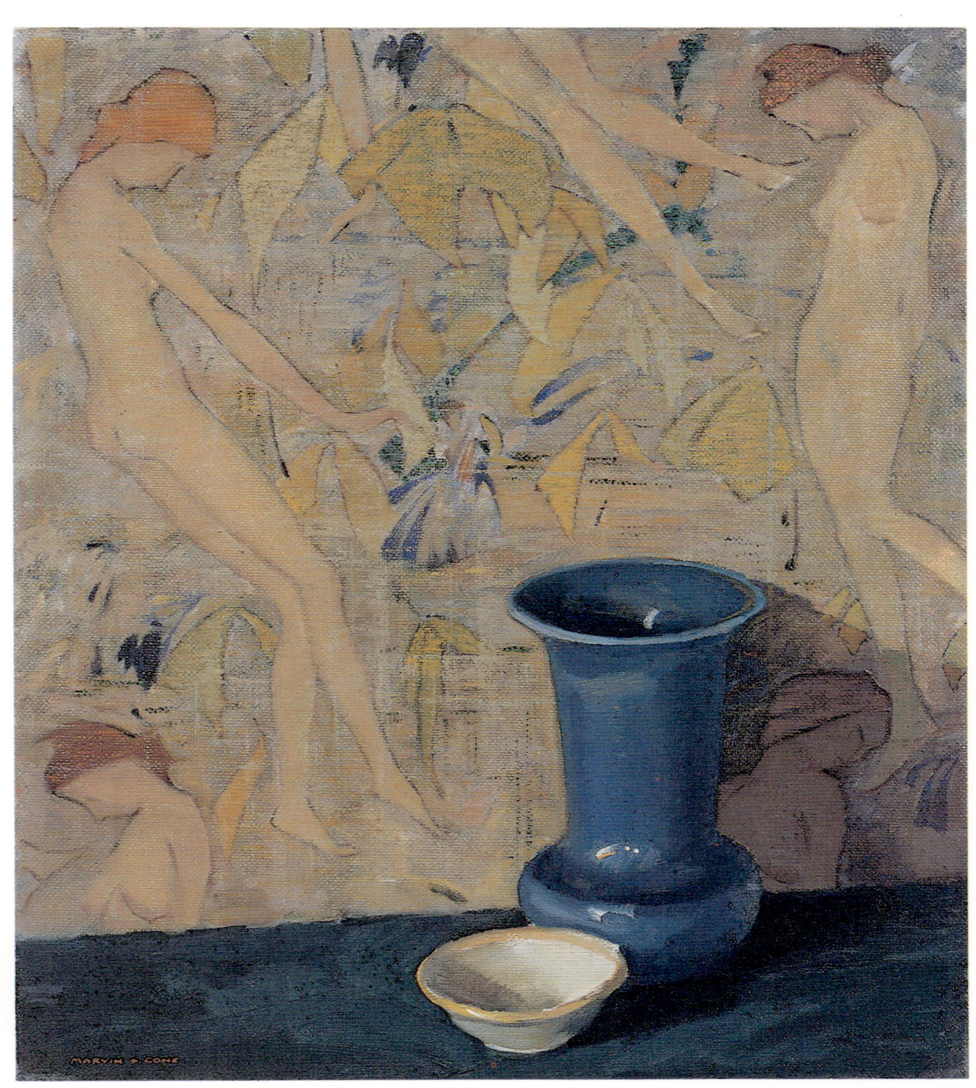


*On Our Mantel,* 1920. Oil on canvas, 18″ x 16″. (Cedar Rapids Museum of Art; Bequest of Miss Nell Cherry, 1969)

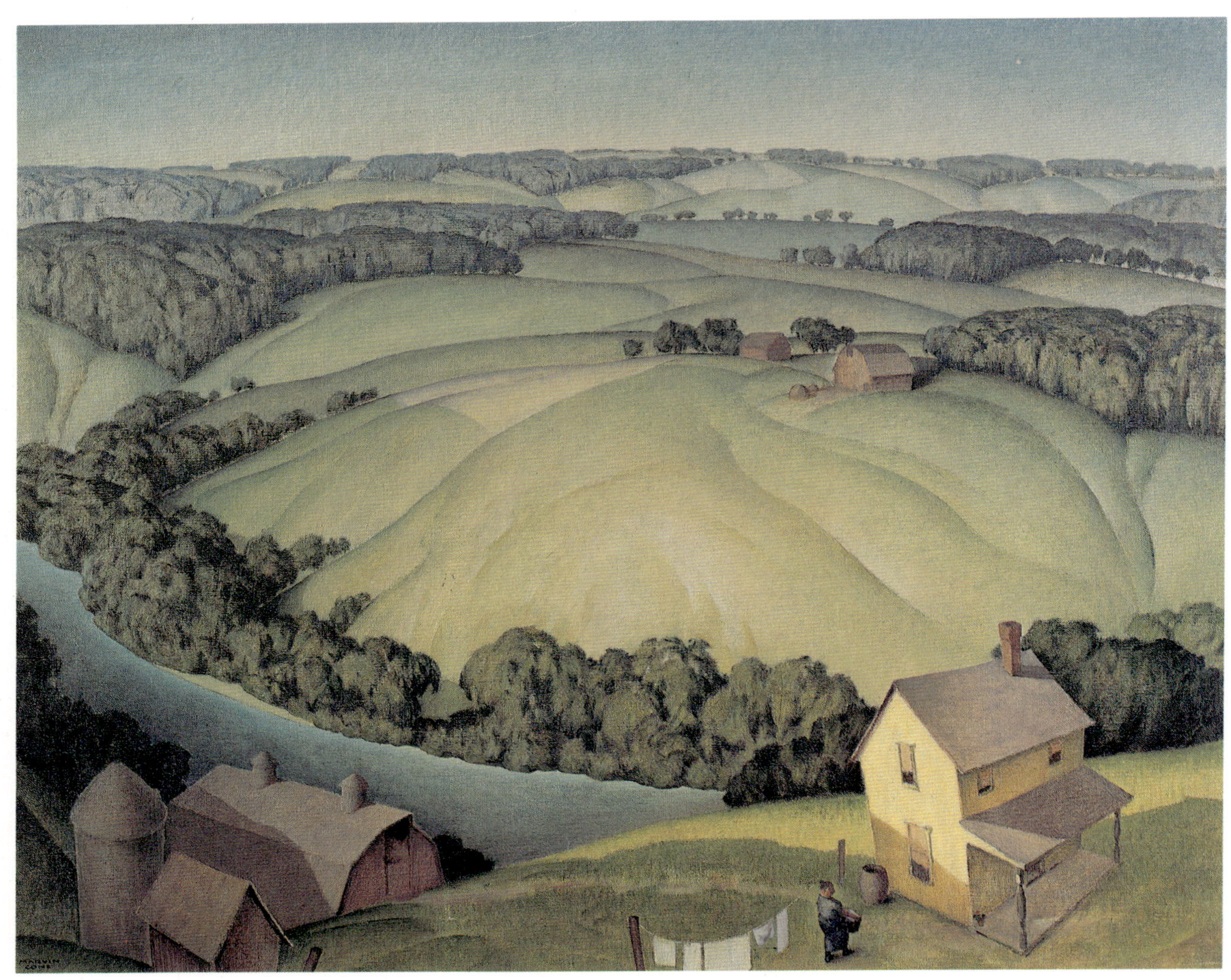

*River Farm,* 1925. Oil on canvas, 24″ x 30″. (Coe College, Cedar Rapids)

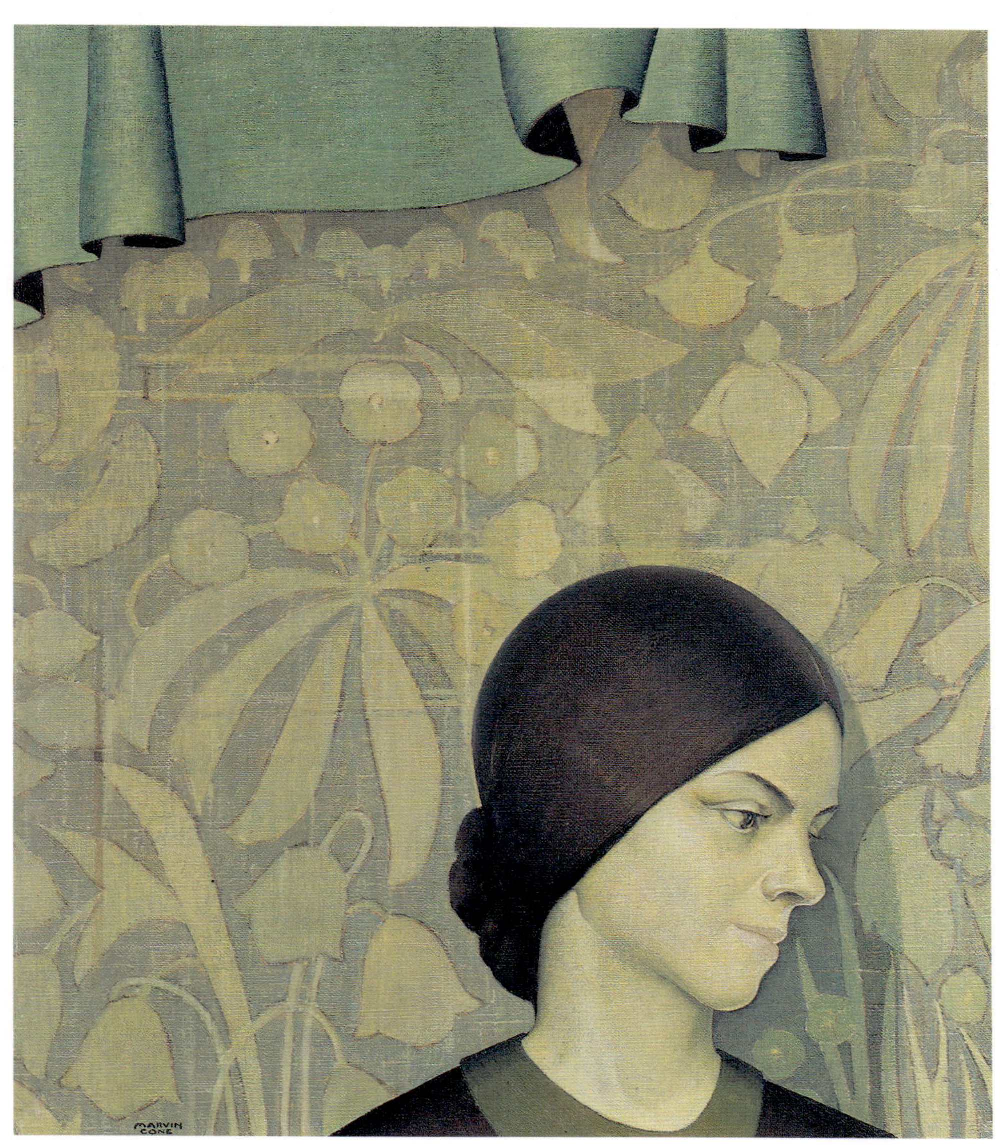


*Color Arrangement—Winnifred,* 1928. Oil on canvas, 20″ x 18″. (Collection of Winnifred Cone)

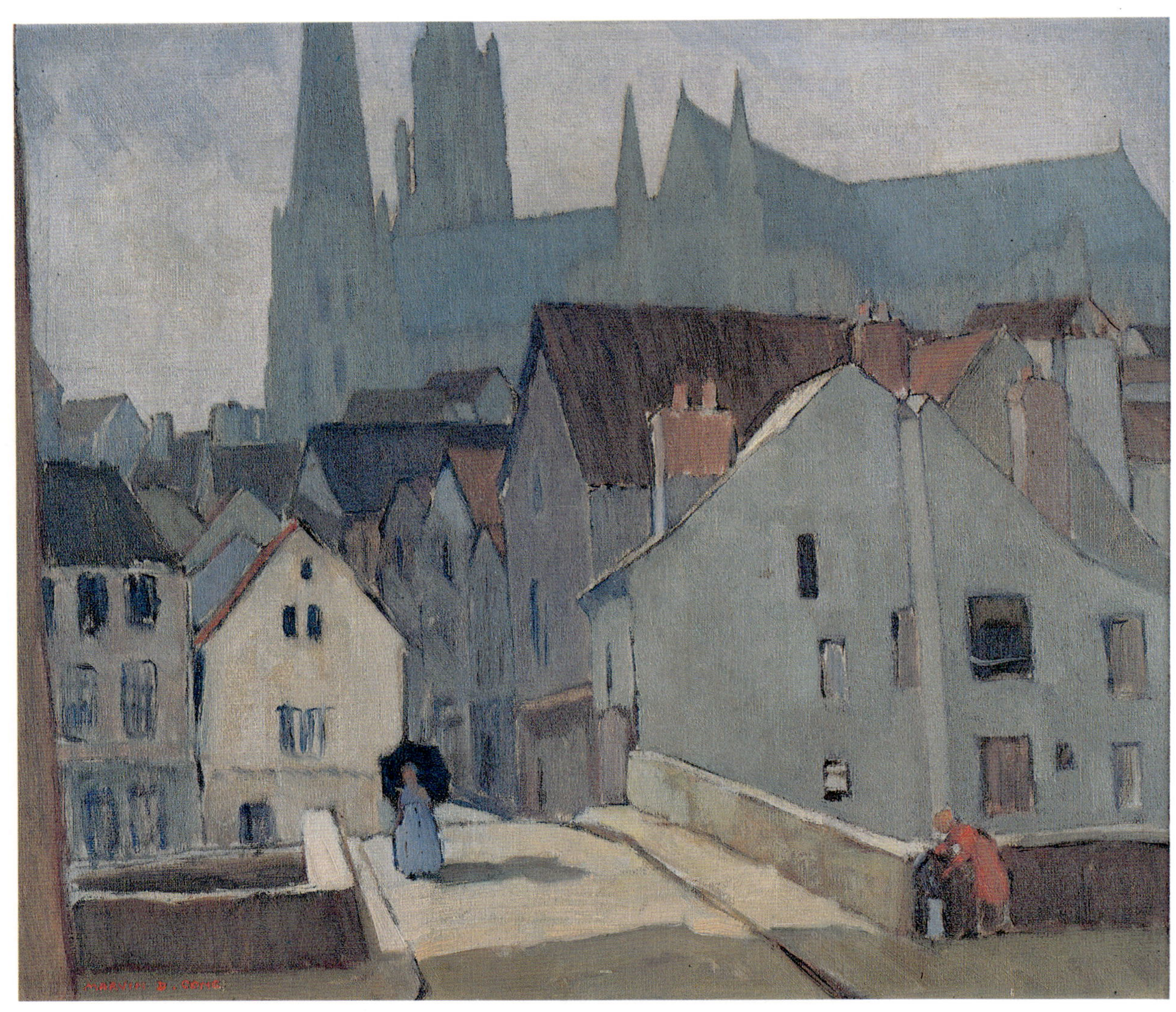

*Chartres*, 1929. Oil on canvas board, 13″ x 15″. (Collection of Mr. and Mrs. Arthur A. Collins)

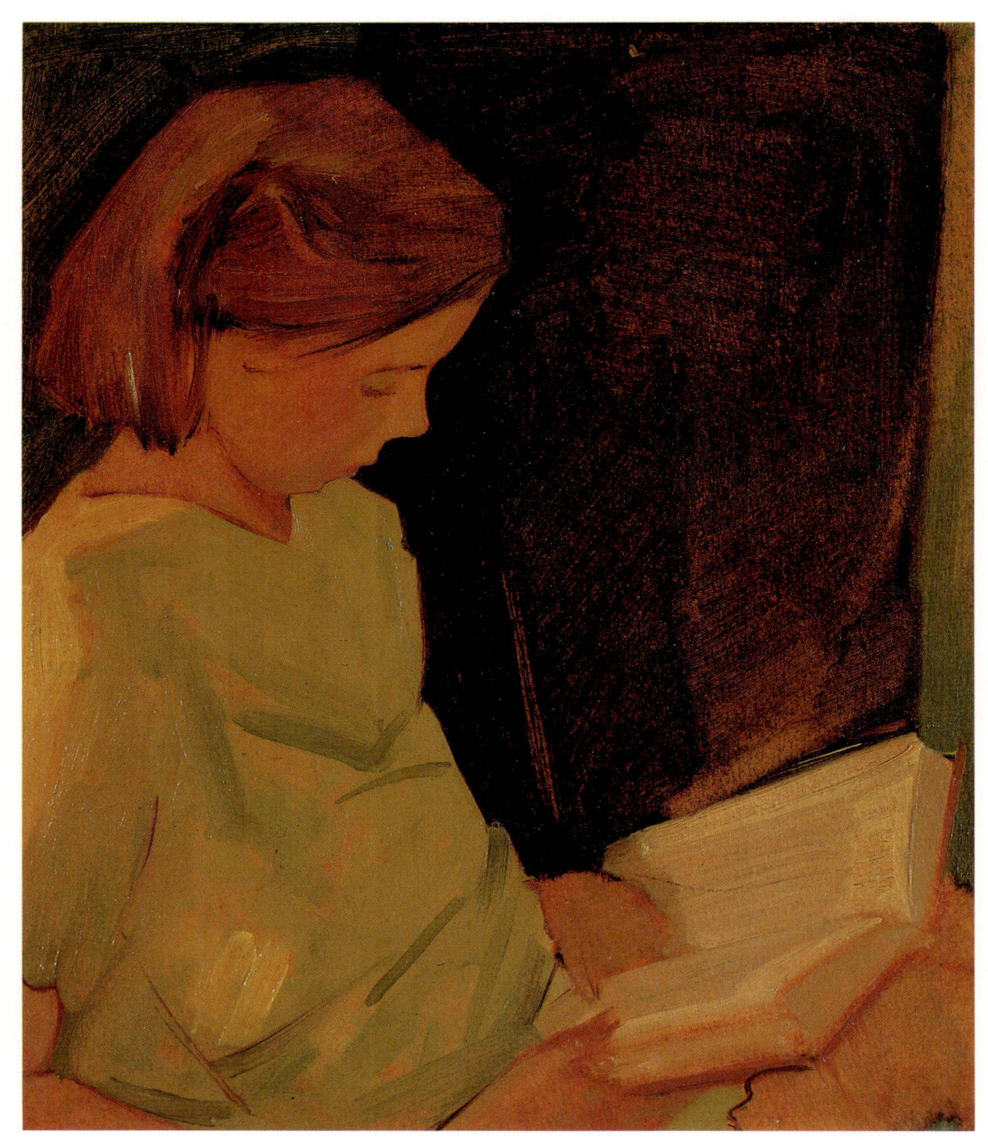

*Doris Reading a Book,* 1929. Oil on panel, 15″ x 13″. (Collection of Winnifred Cone)

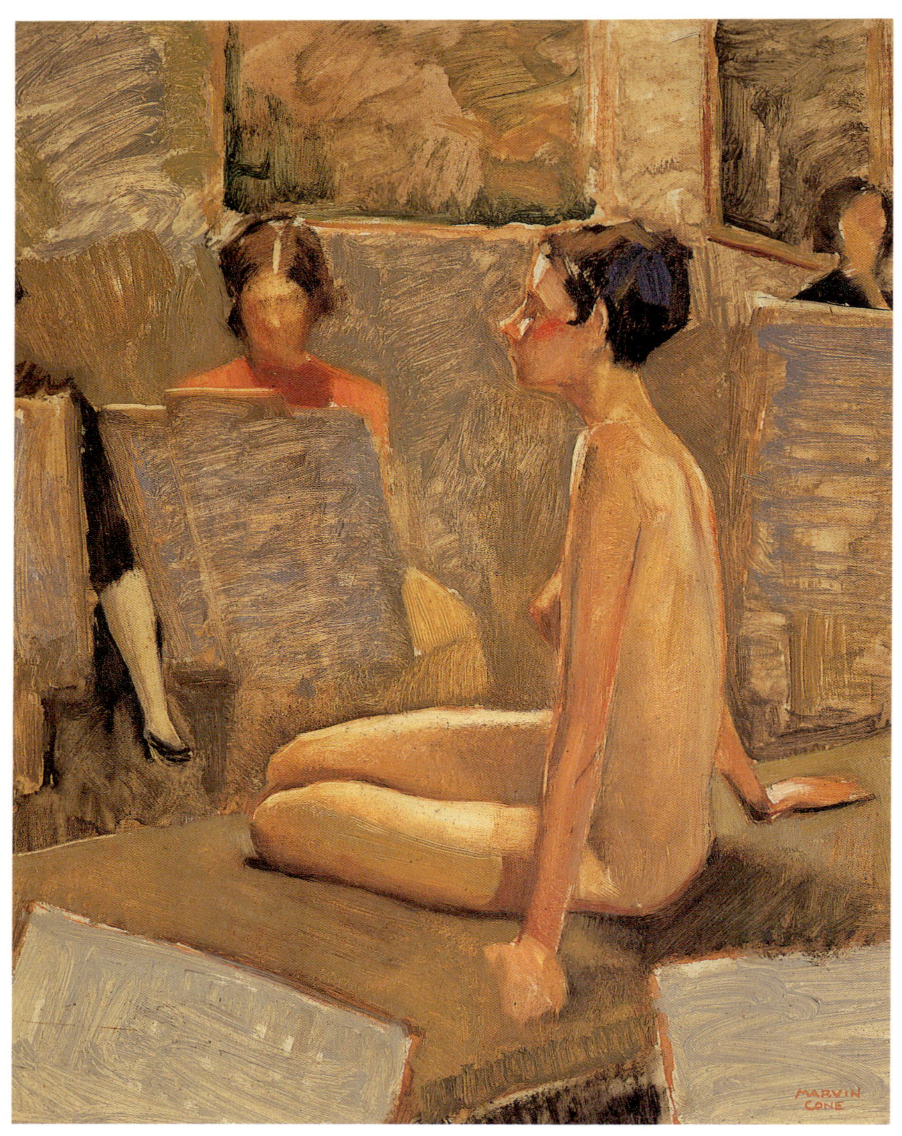


*In the Studio,* 1929. Oil on panel, 18″ x 15″. (Cedar Rapids Museum of Art; Gift of Winnifred Cone and Family)

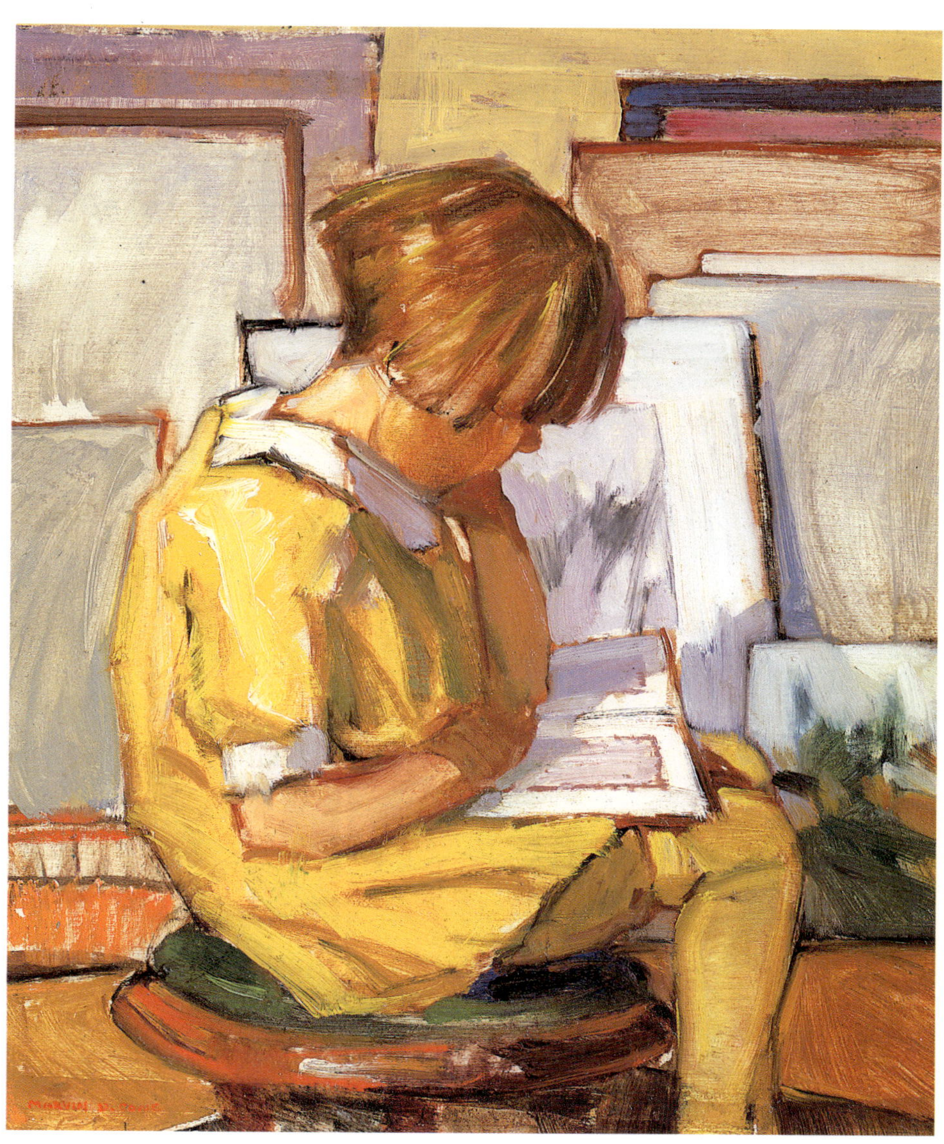

*A Little Girl,* 1929. Oil on panel, 15″ x 13″. (Cedar Rapids Museum of Art; Gift of Keith DeBolt)

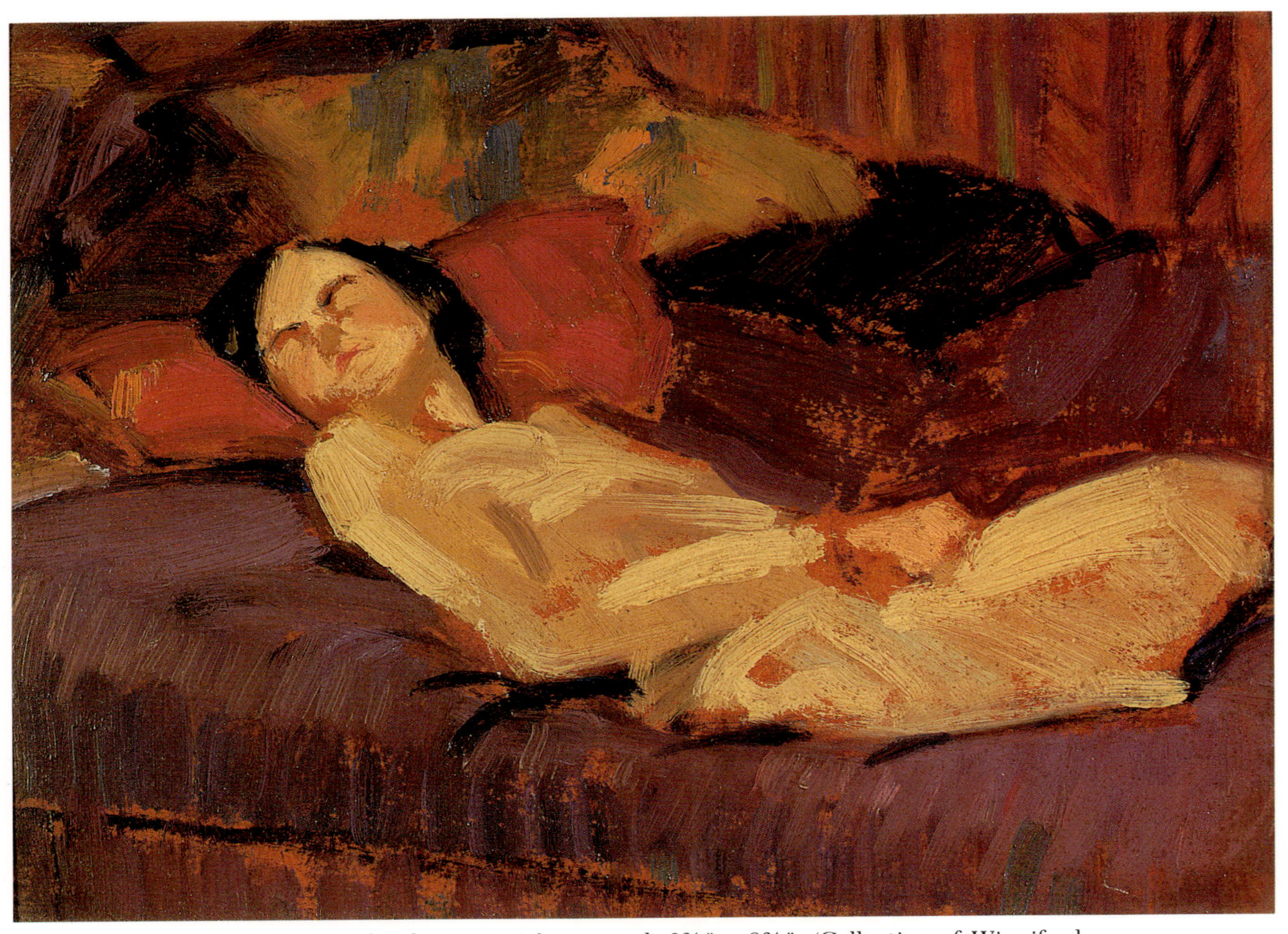

*Paris Studio Sketch*, 1929. Oil on panel, 6⅜″ x 8¾″. (Collection of Winnifred Cone)

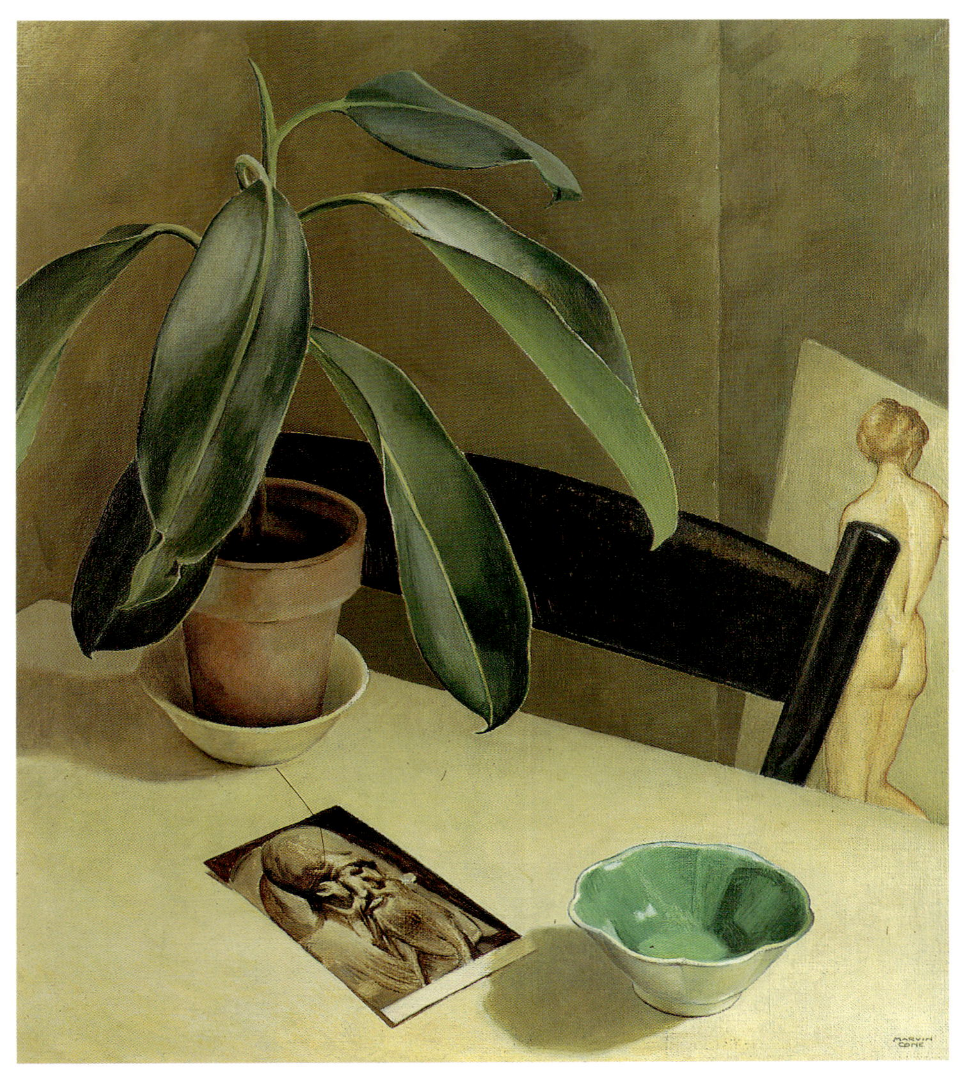


*Passage des Postes, Paris,* 1929. Oil on canvas, 20″ x 18″. (Collection of Mrs. James Cooper)

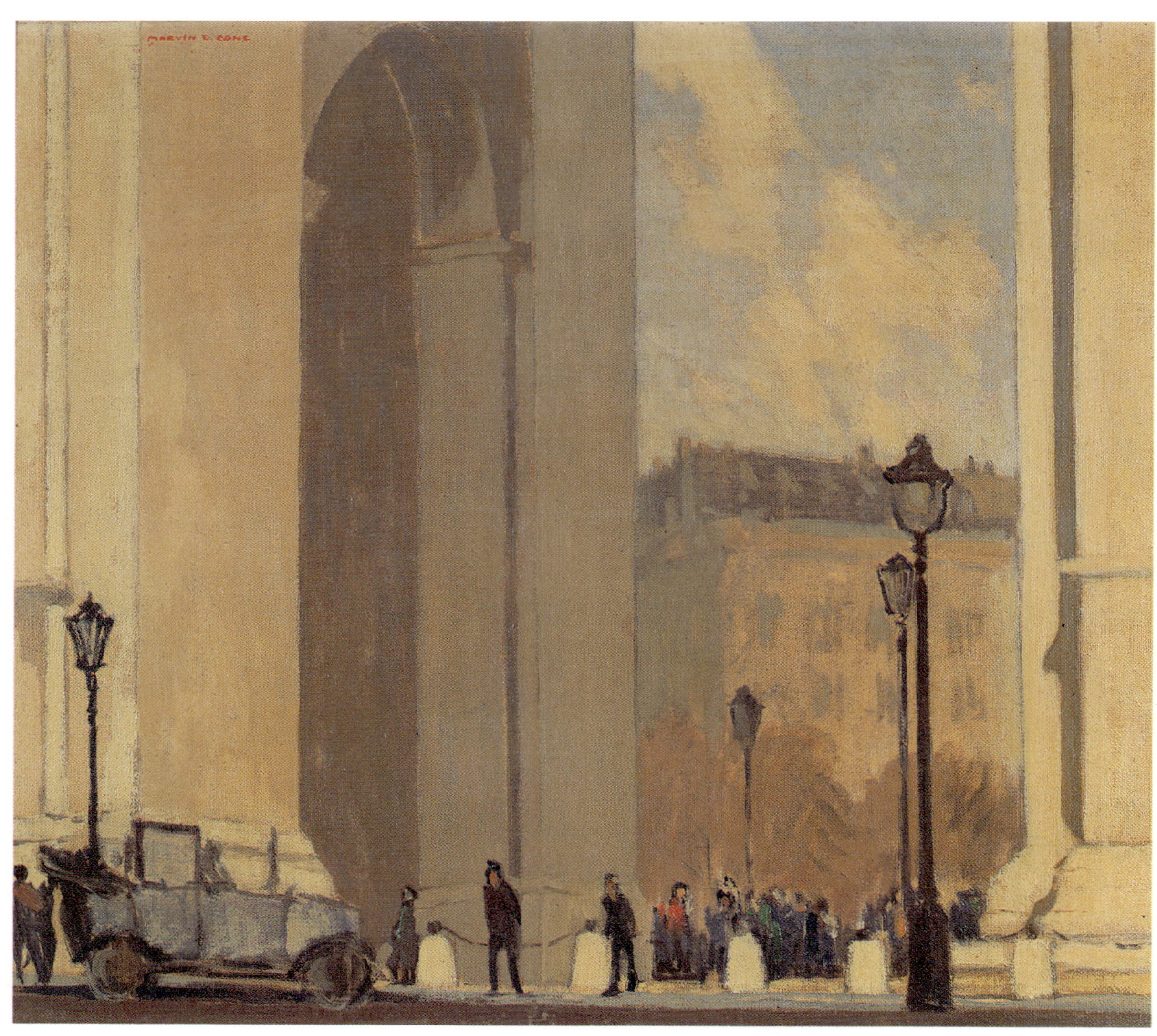


*Under the Arch of Triumph, Paris,* 1929. Oil on canvas, 13″ x 15″. (Coe College, Cedar Rapids)

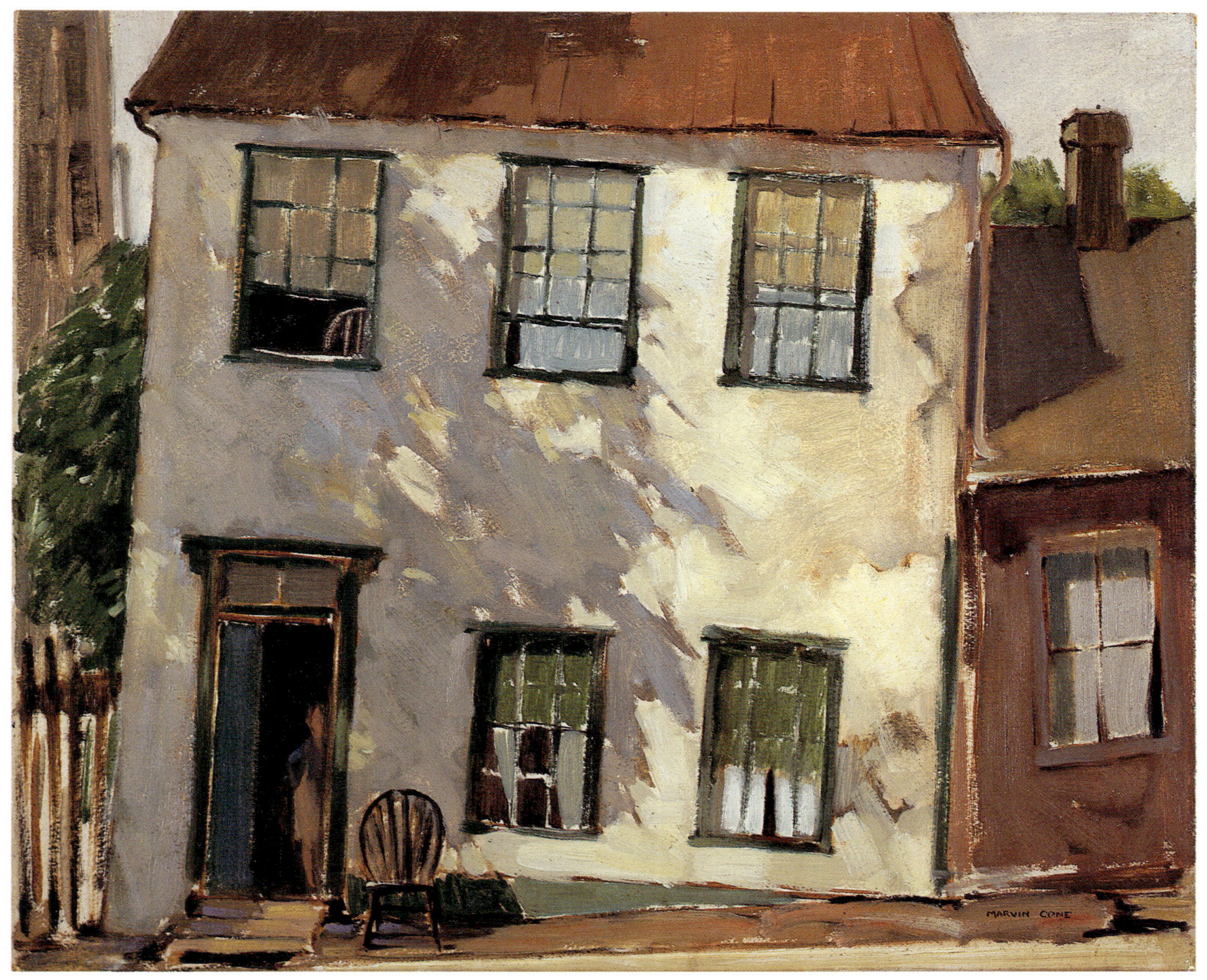


*Old House, Toronto,* c. 1930. Oil on canvas, 15″ x 18″. (Collection of Mr. and Mrs. D. William Coppock)

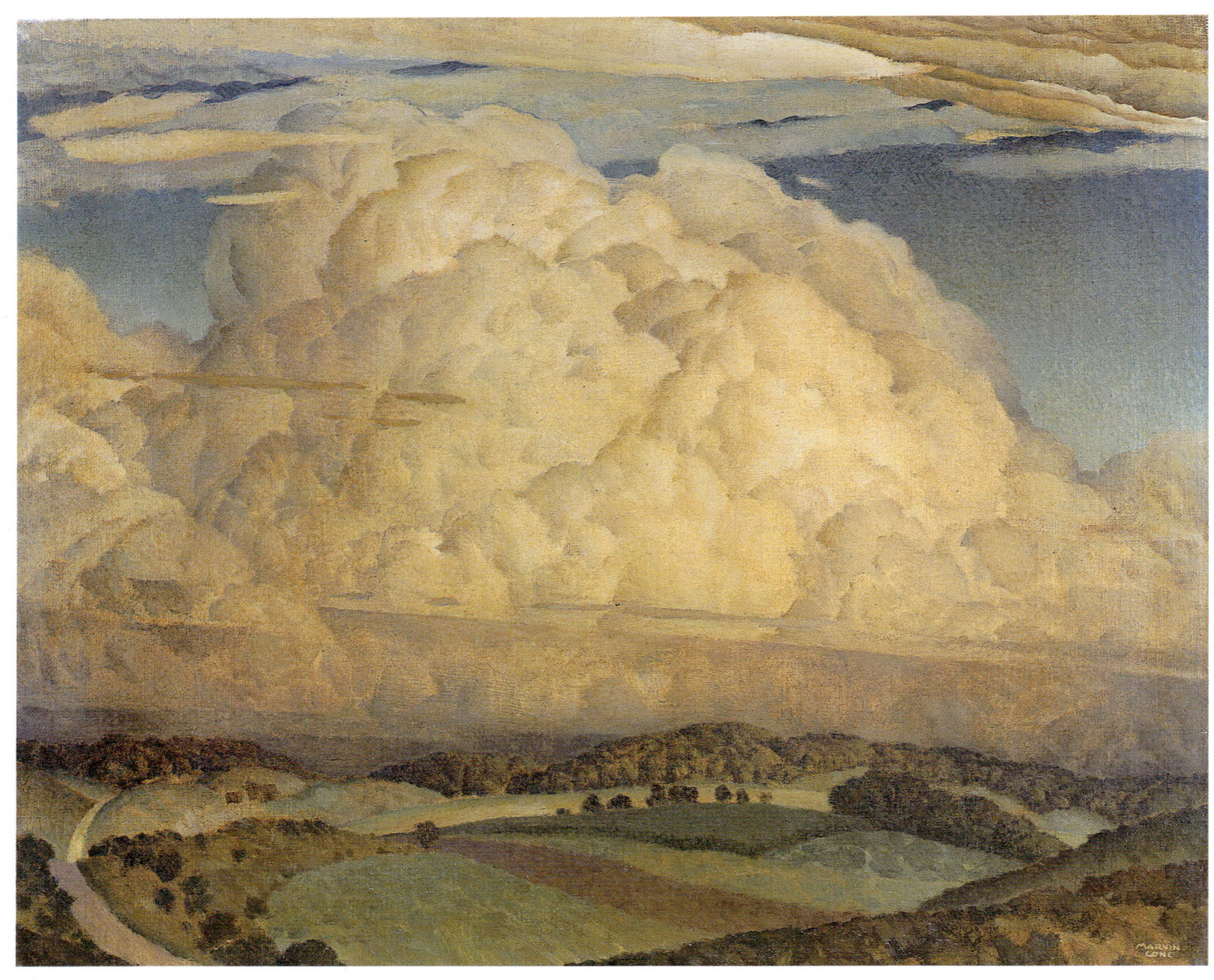


*July Clouds,* 1931. Oil on canvas, 18⅛″ x 22⅛″. (Cedar Rapids Museum of Art; Gift of Happy Young and John B. Turner II, 1983)

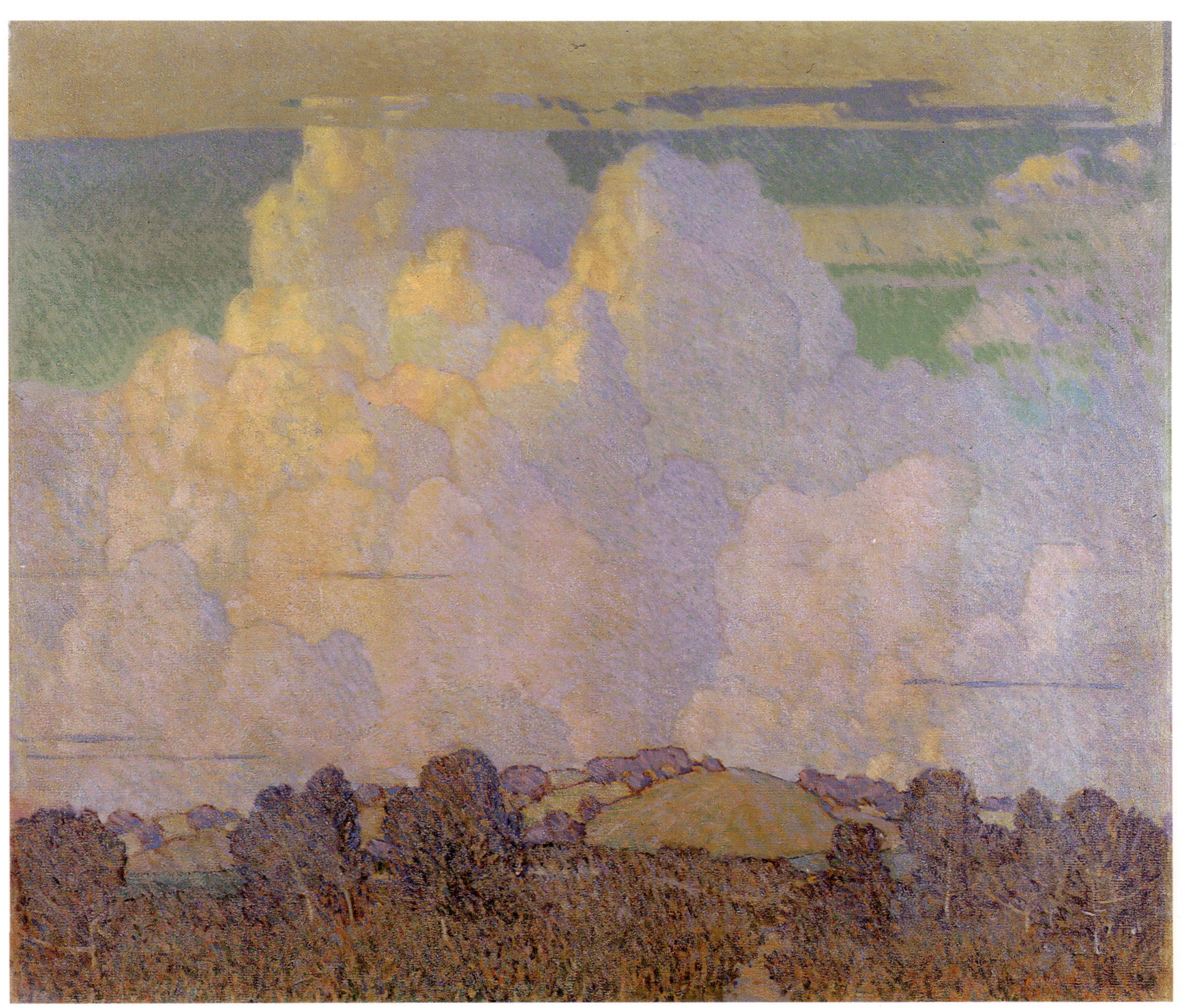

*Tranquillity,* 1931. Oil on canvas, 32″ x 28″. (Cedar Rapids Museum of Art; Cedar Rapids Area Chamber of Commerce Collection)

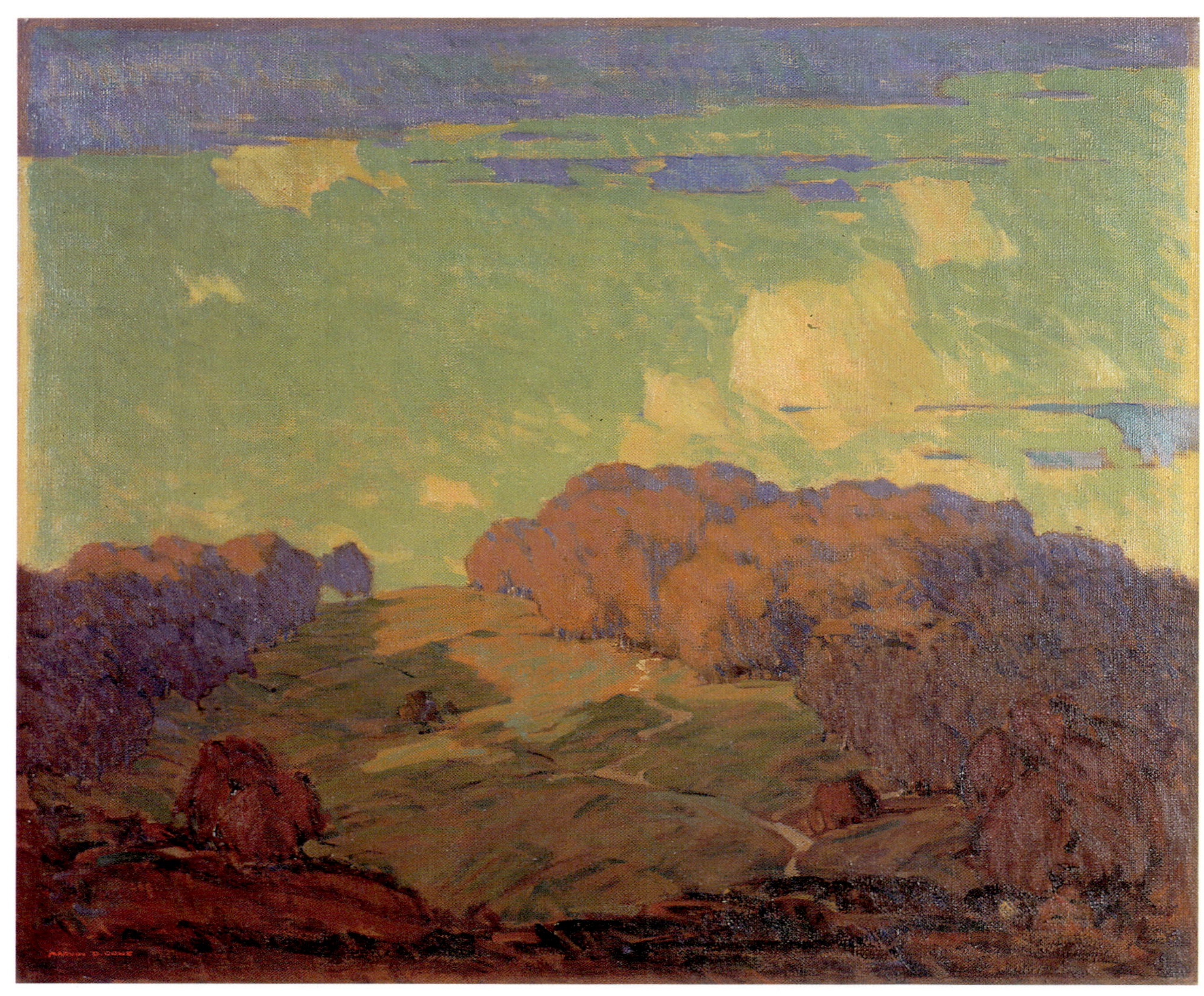

*Autumn Hillside,* 1931. Oil on canvas, 20″ x 23¼″. (Cedar Rapids Museum of Art; Iowa Electric Light & Power Company Collection)

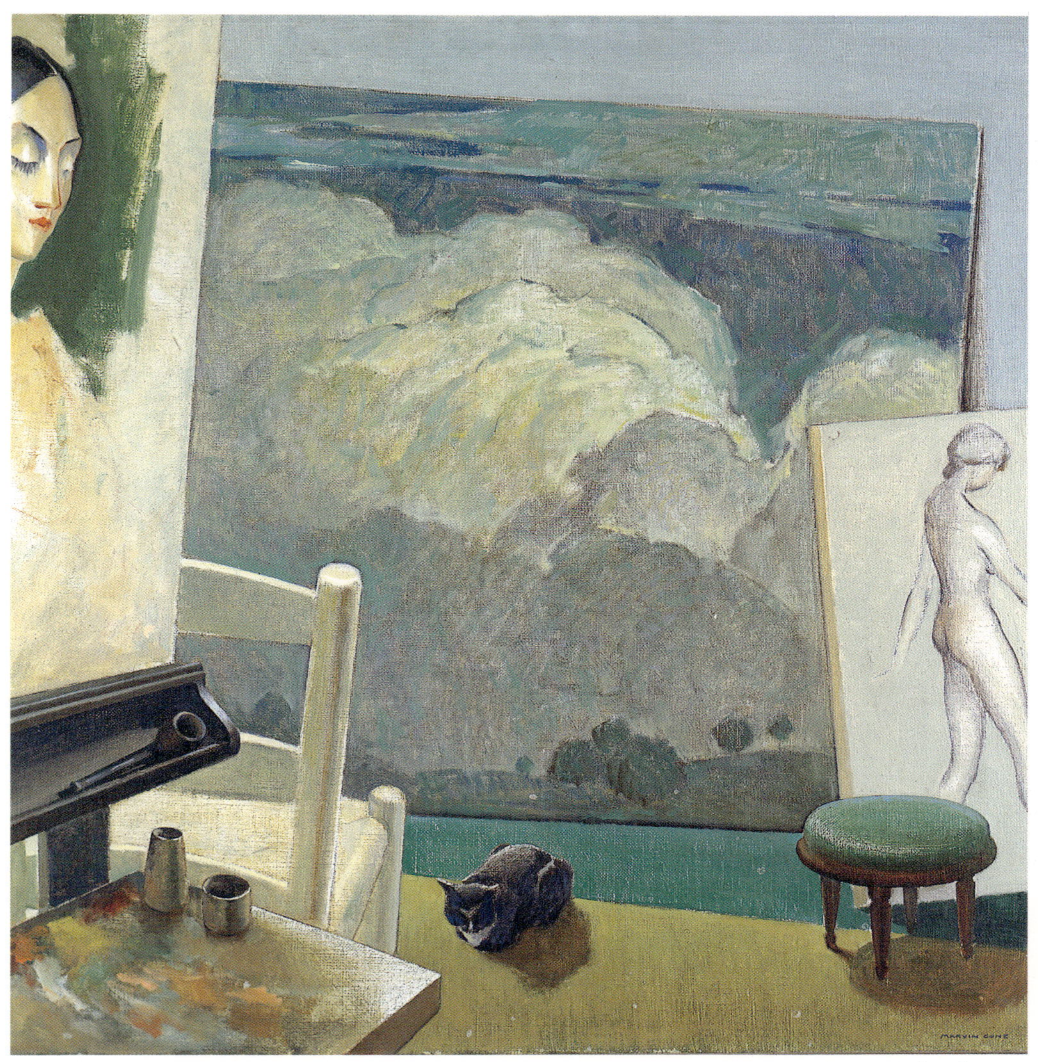


*Achmed,* 1933. Oil on canvas, 22″ x 22″. (Cedar Rapids Museum of Art; Gift of Winnifred Cone and Family, and Museum Purchase, 1982)

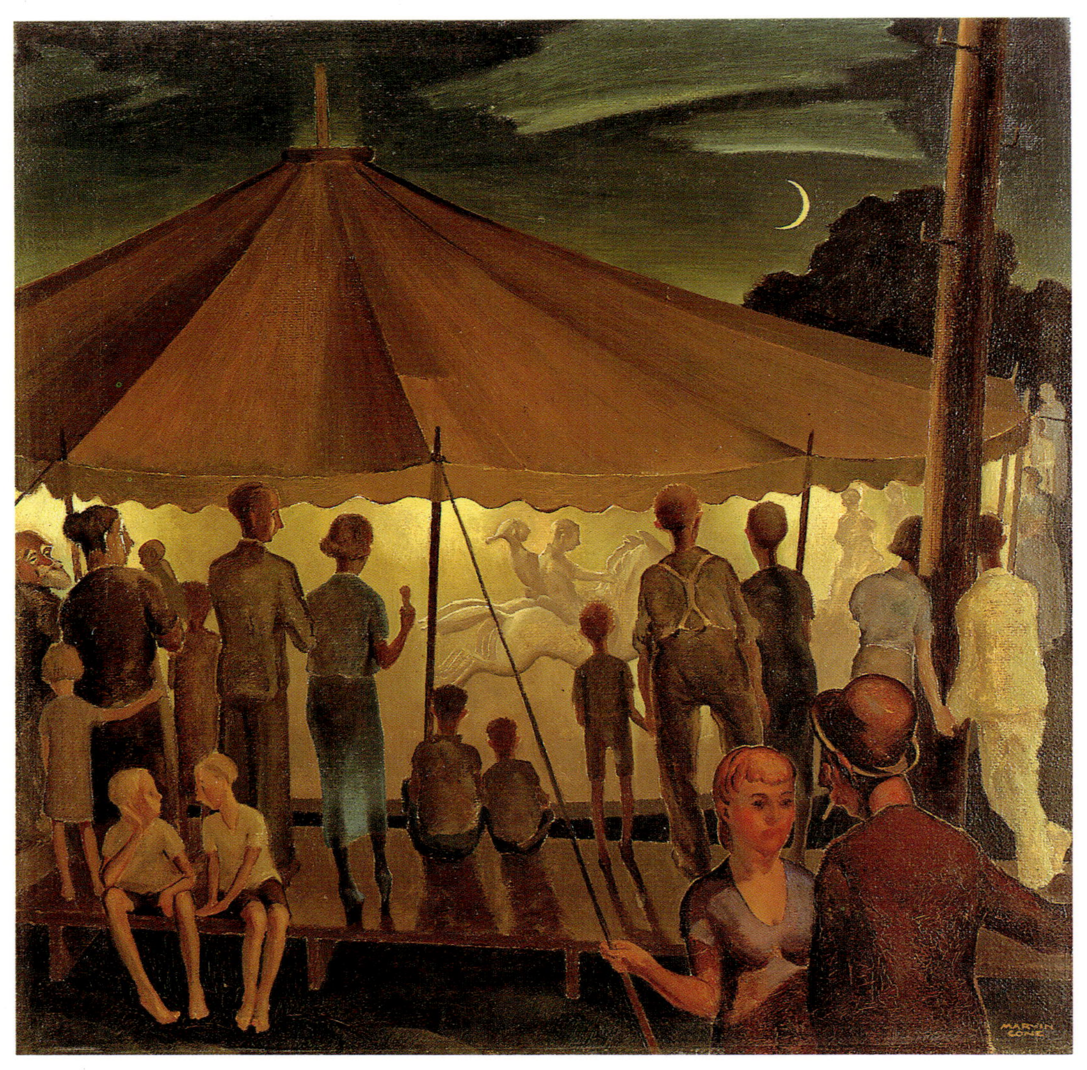


*Merry-Go-Round,* 1934. Oil on canvas, 18¼″ x 18¼″. (Private collection)

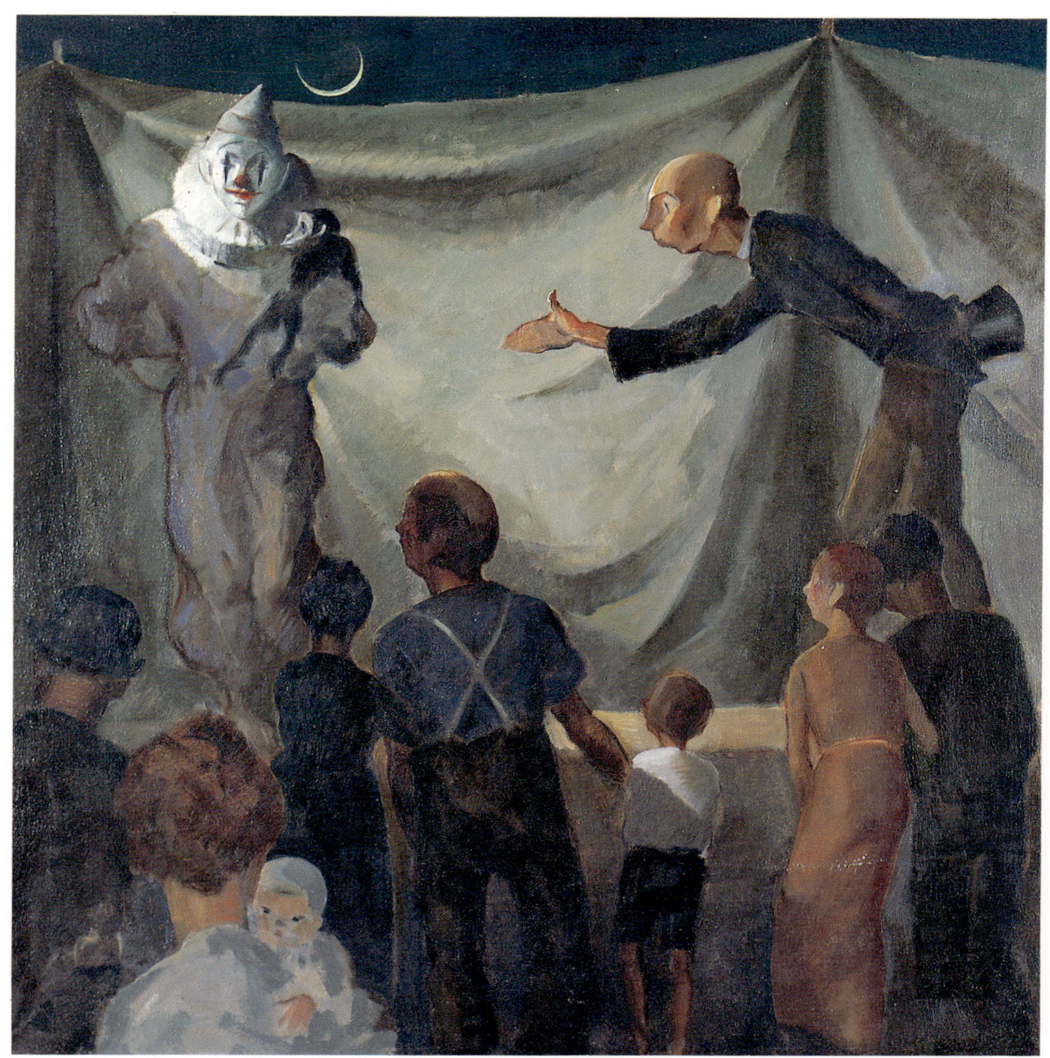

*Two Clowns with White Face,* c. 1935. Oil on canvas, 24″ x 24″. (Cedar Rapids Museum of Art; Gift of Winnifred Cone and Family, and Museum Purchase, 1982)

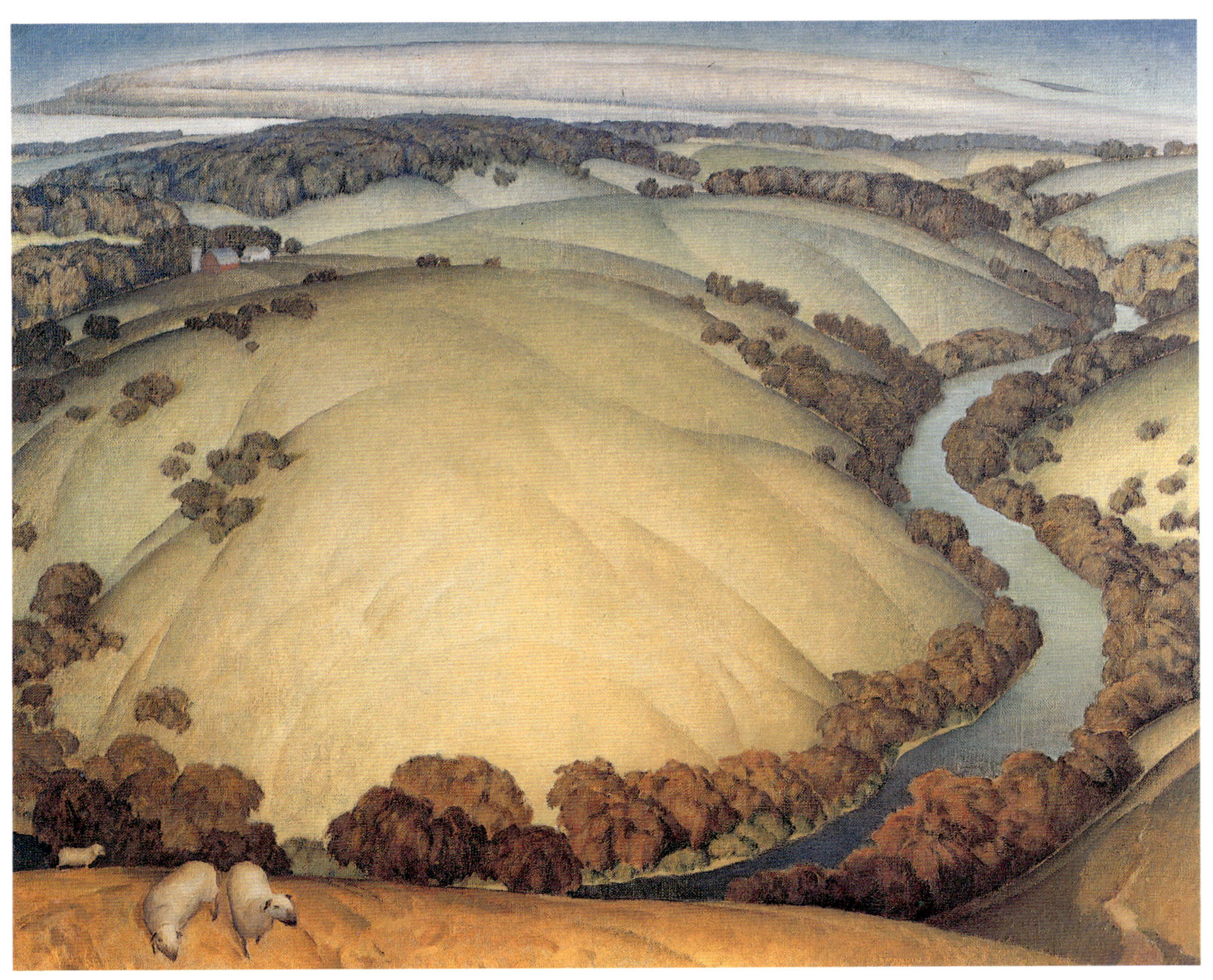

*River Bend No. 5,* 1936. Oil on canvas, 24″ x 30″. (Cedar Rapids Museum of Art; Gift of Isobel Howell Brown)

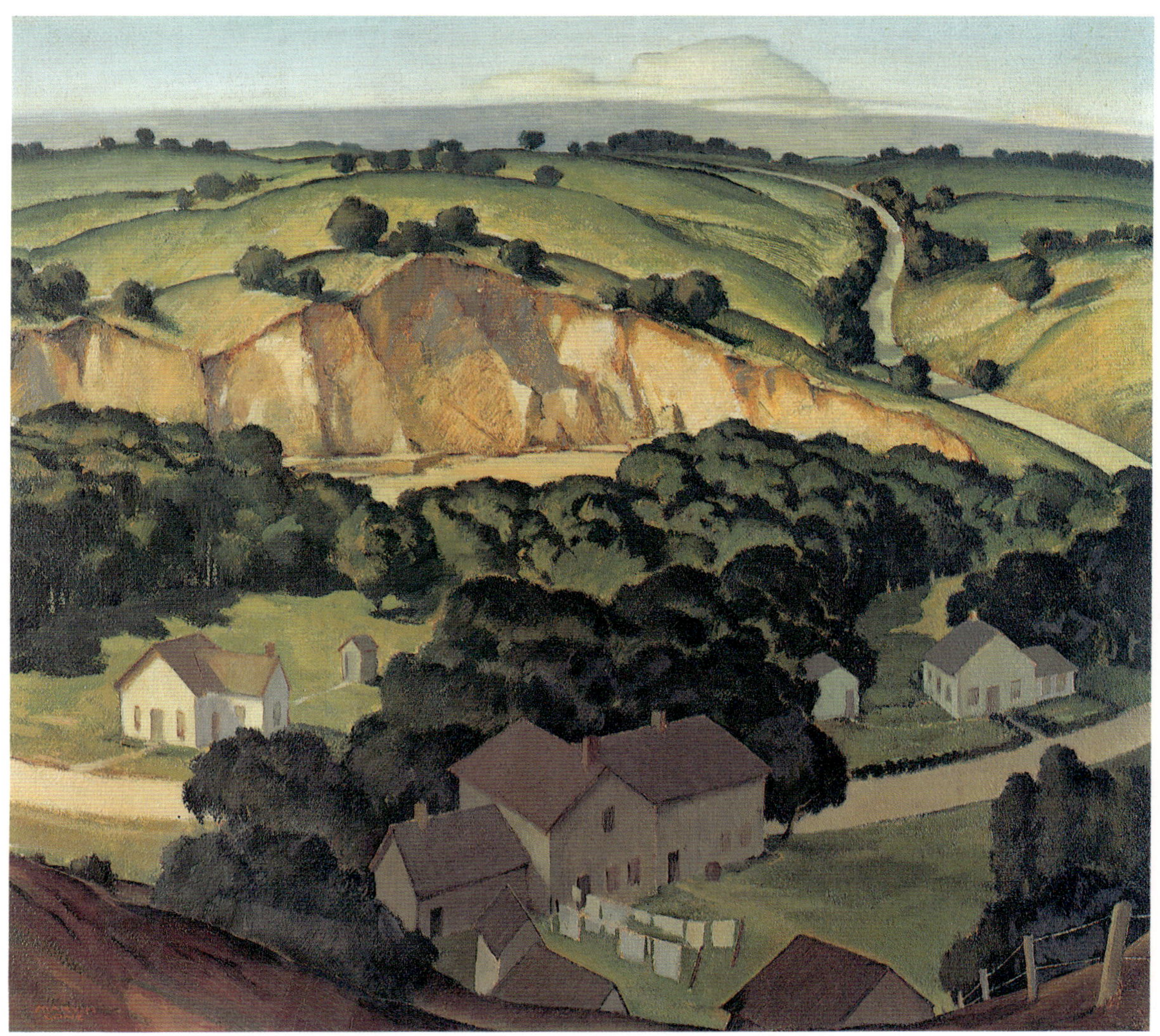

*Old Quarry, Stone City* (sketch), 1936. Oil on canvas, 18″ x 20″. (Cedar Rapids Museum of Art; Delta, Delta, Delta Alumni Collection)

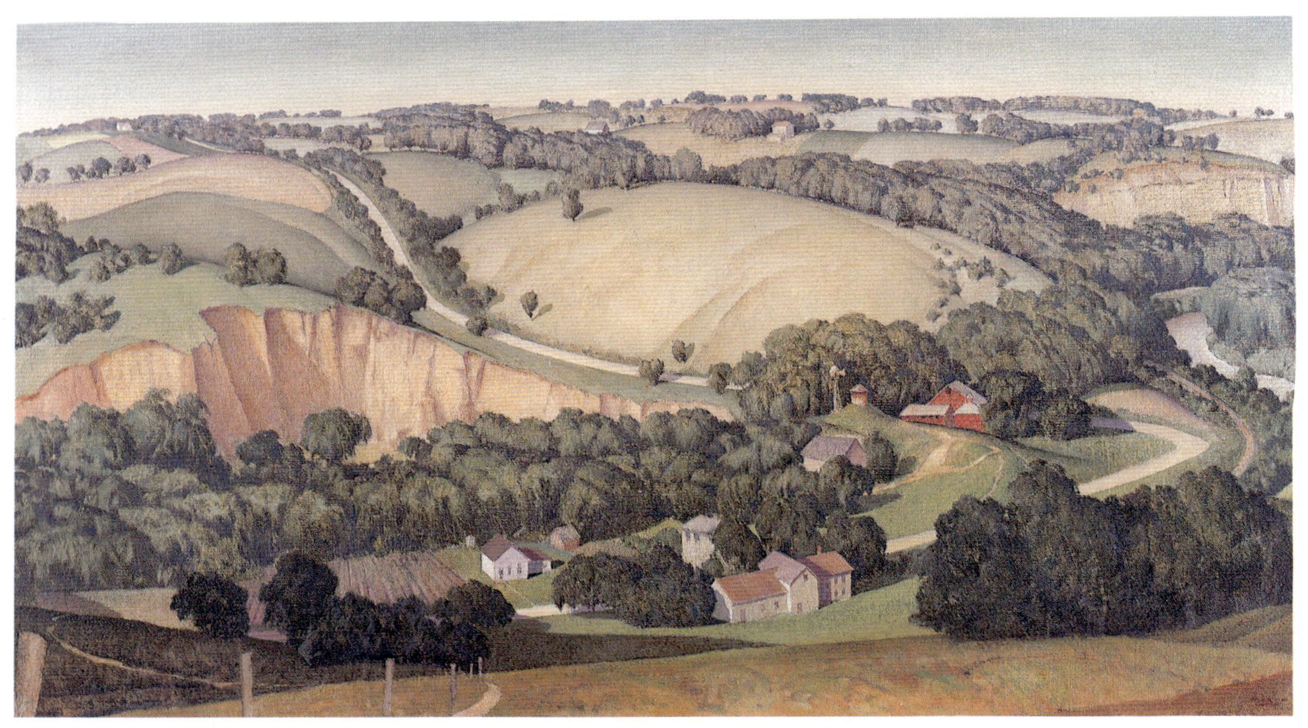

*Old Quarry, Stone City,* 1937. Oil on canvas, 20″ x 36″. (Collection of Mr. and Mrs. Robert Armstrong)

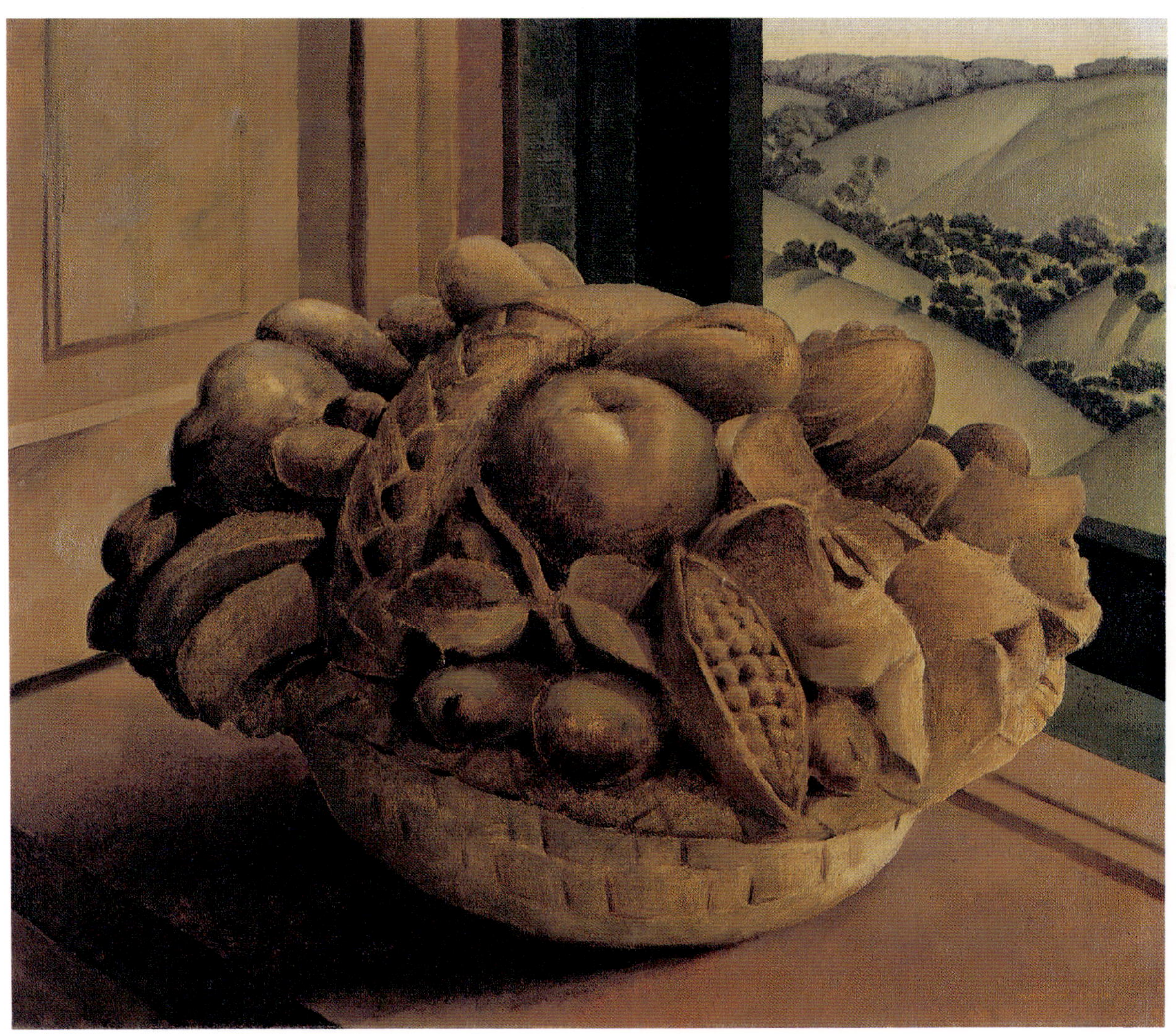

*Stone Fruit,* 1937. Oil on canvas, 18″ x 20″. (Cedar Rapids Museum of Art; Gift of Happy Young and John B. Turner II, 1983)

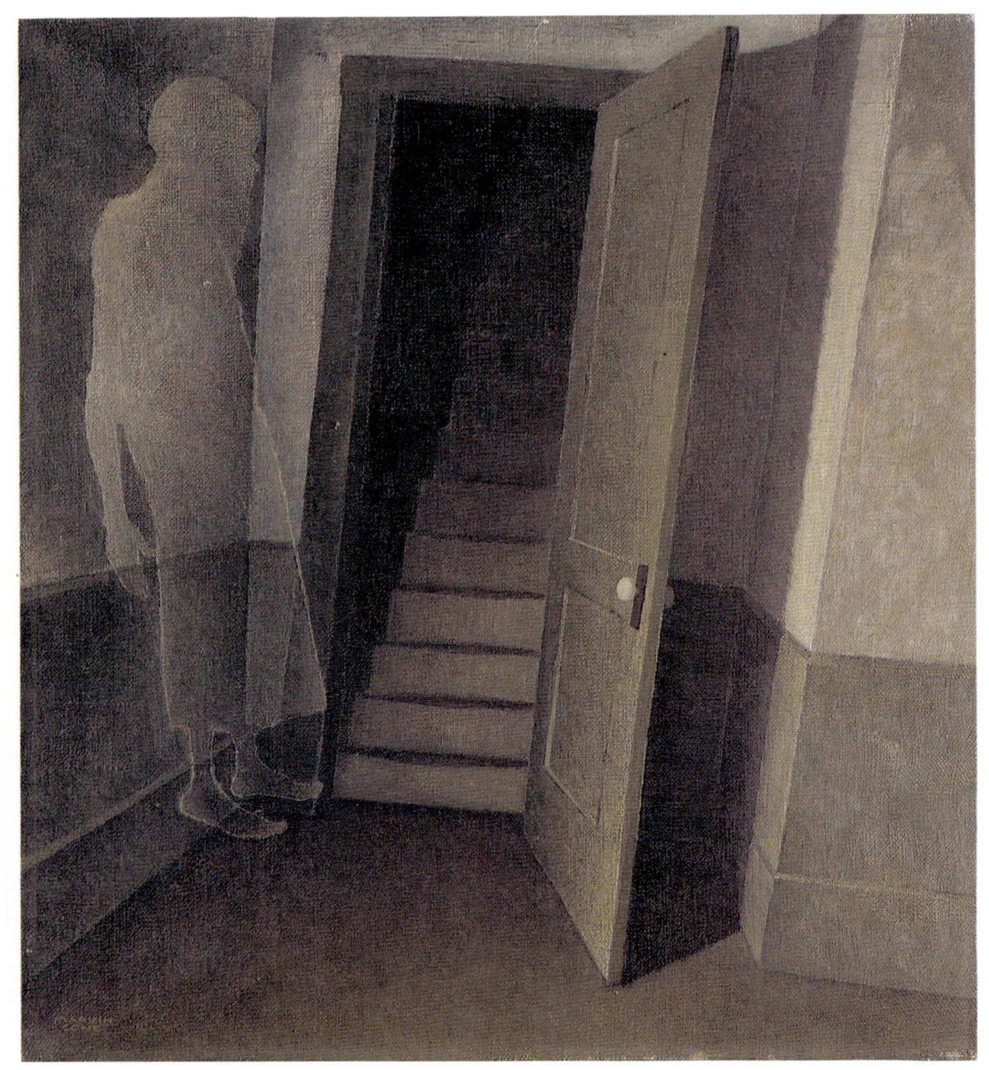

*Anniversary,* 1938. Oil on canvas, 18″ x 16″. (Cedar Rapids Museum of Art; Gift of Winnifred Cone and Family, and Museum Purchase, 1982)

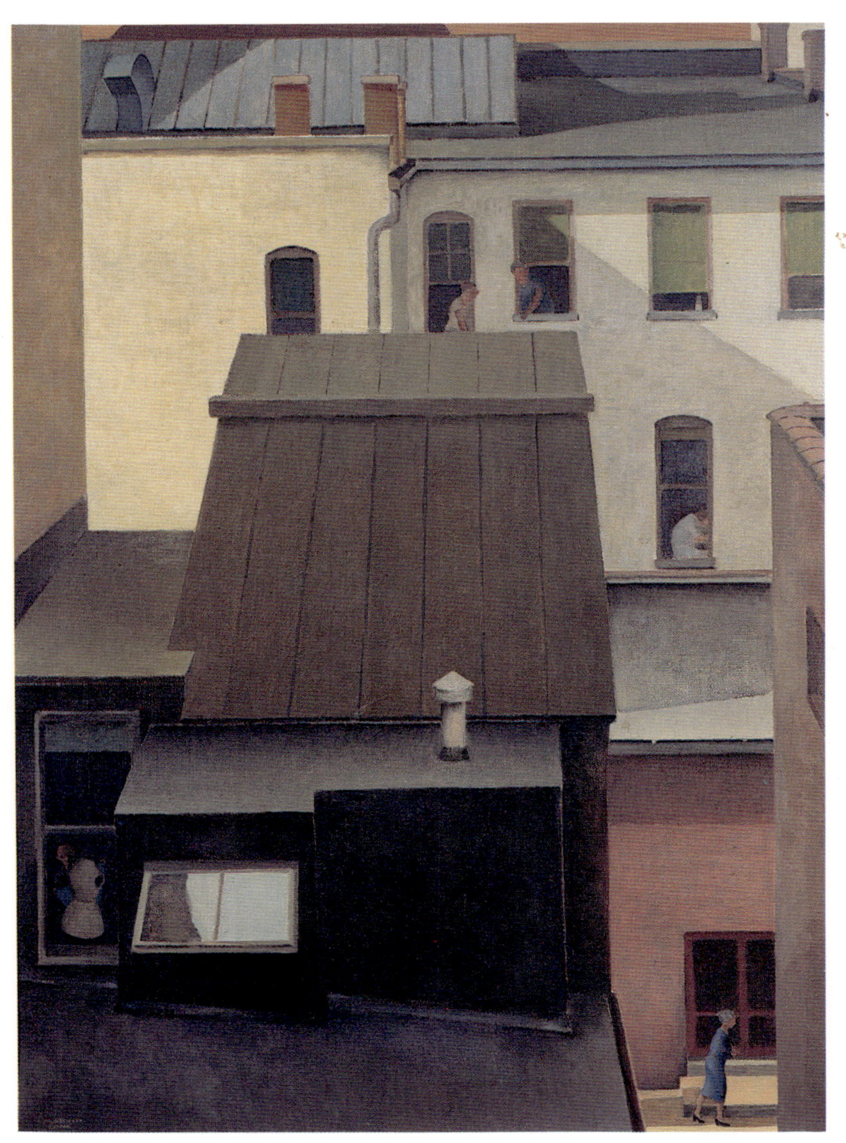

*Davies' Dummy,* 1938. Oil on canvas, 30″ x 22″. (Collection of Winnifred Cone)

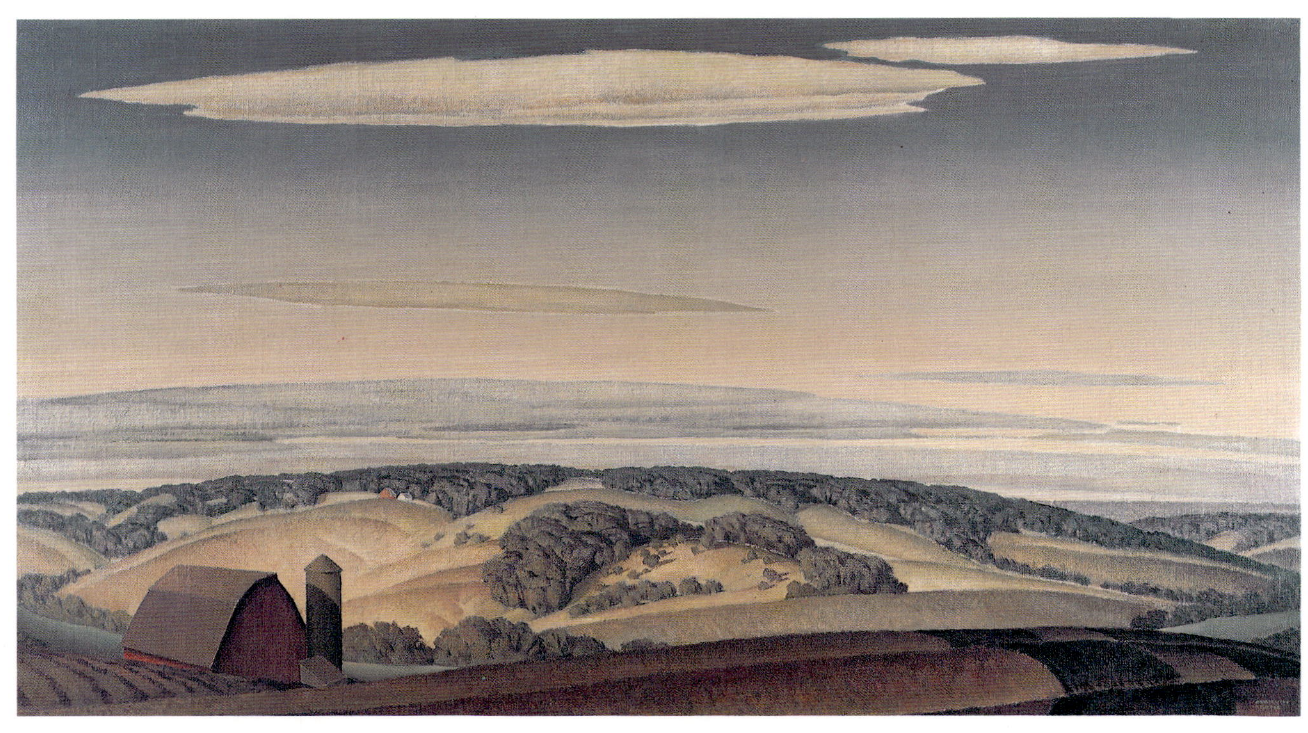

*Prairie Parallels,* 1938–1939. Oil on canvas, 20″ x 36″. (Collection of Gordon Fennell)

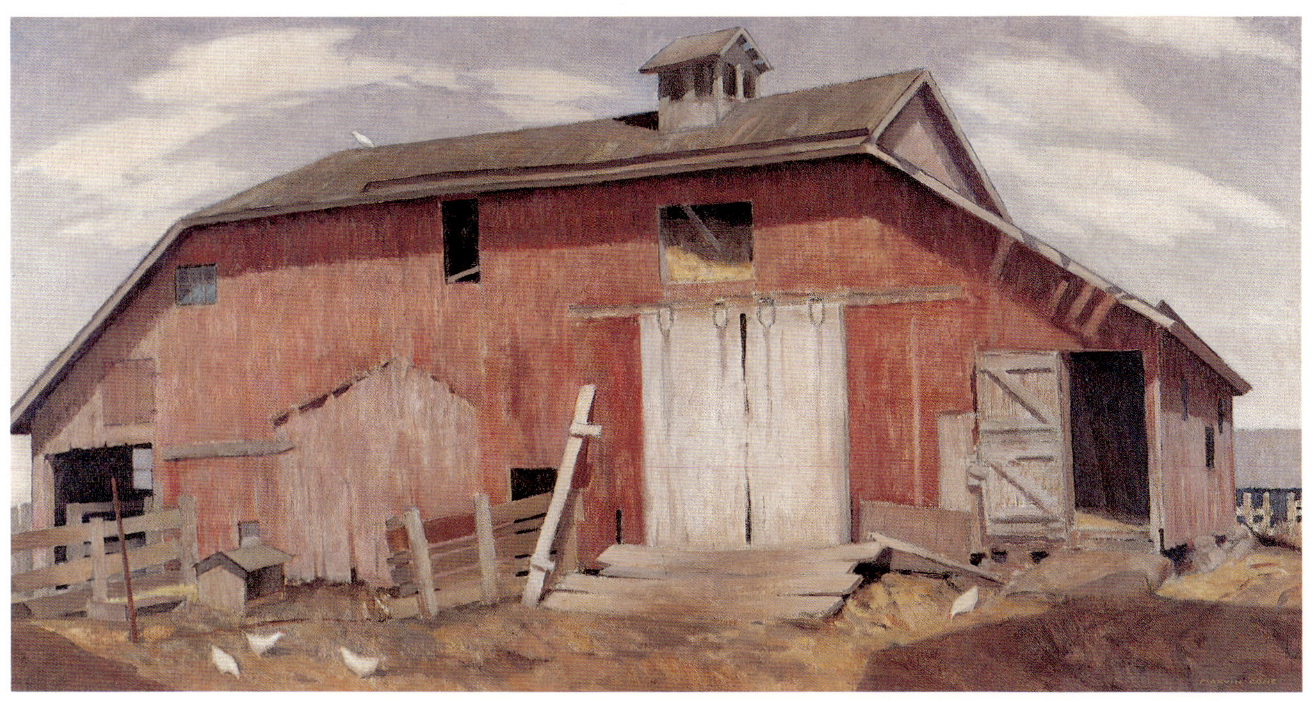

*Old Iowa Barn,* 1938–1939. Oil on canvas, 16″ x 30″. (Cedar Rapids Museum of Art; Art Association Purchase, 1939)

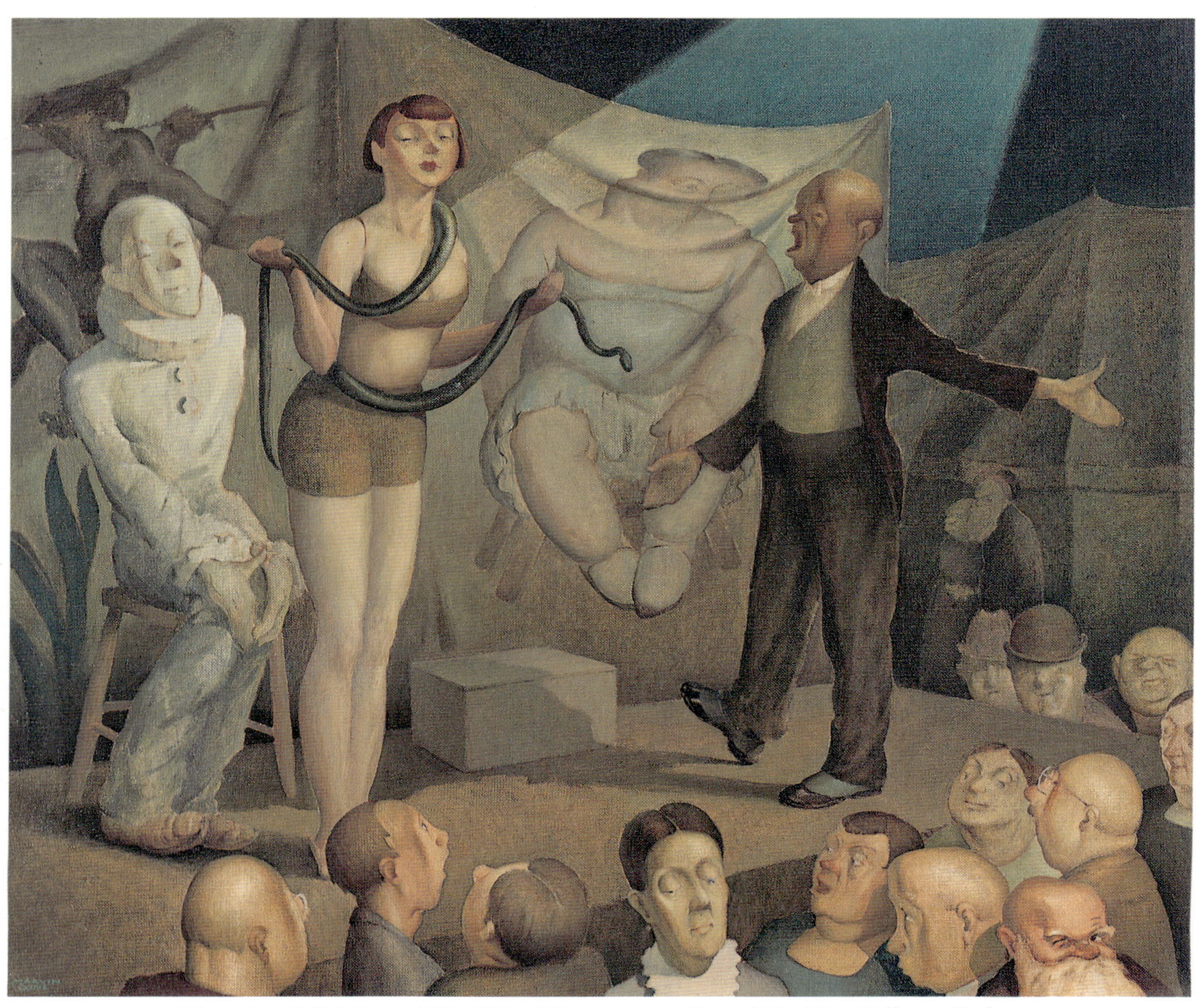

*Educational Exhibit,* 1938–1939. Oil on canvas, 20″ x 24″. (Coe College, Cedar Rapids)

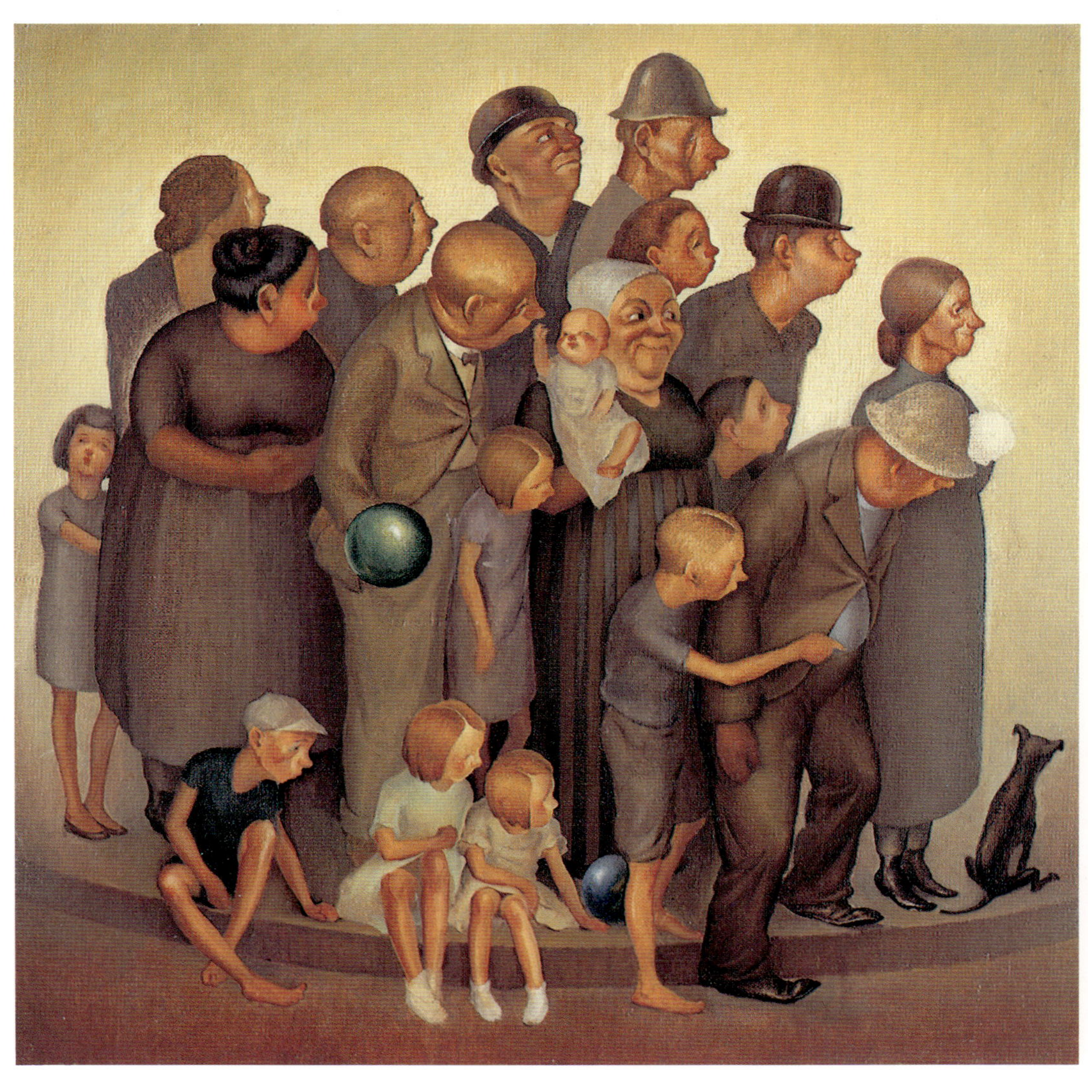

*Waiting for the Parade,* 1938–1939. Oil on canvas, 19¾″ x 19¾″. (Cedar Rapids Museum of Art; Gift of Winnifred Cone and Family, and Museum Purchase, 1983)

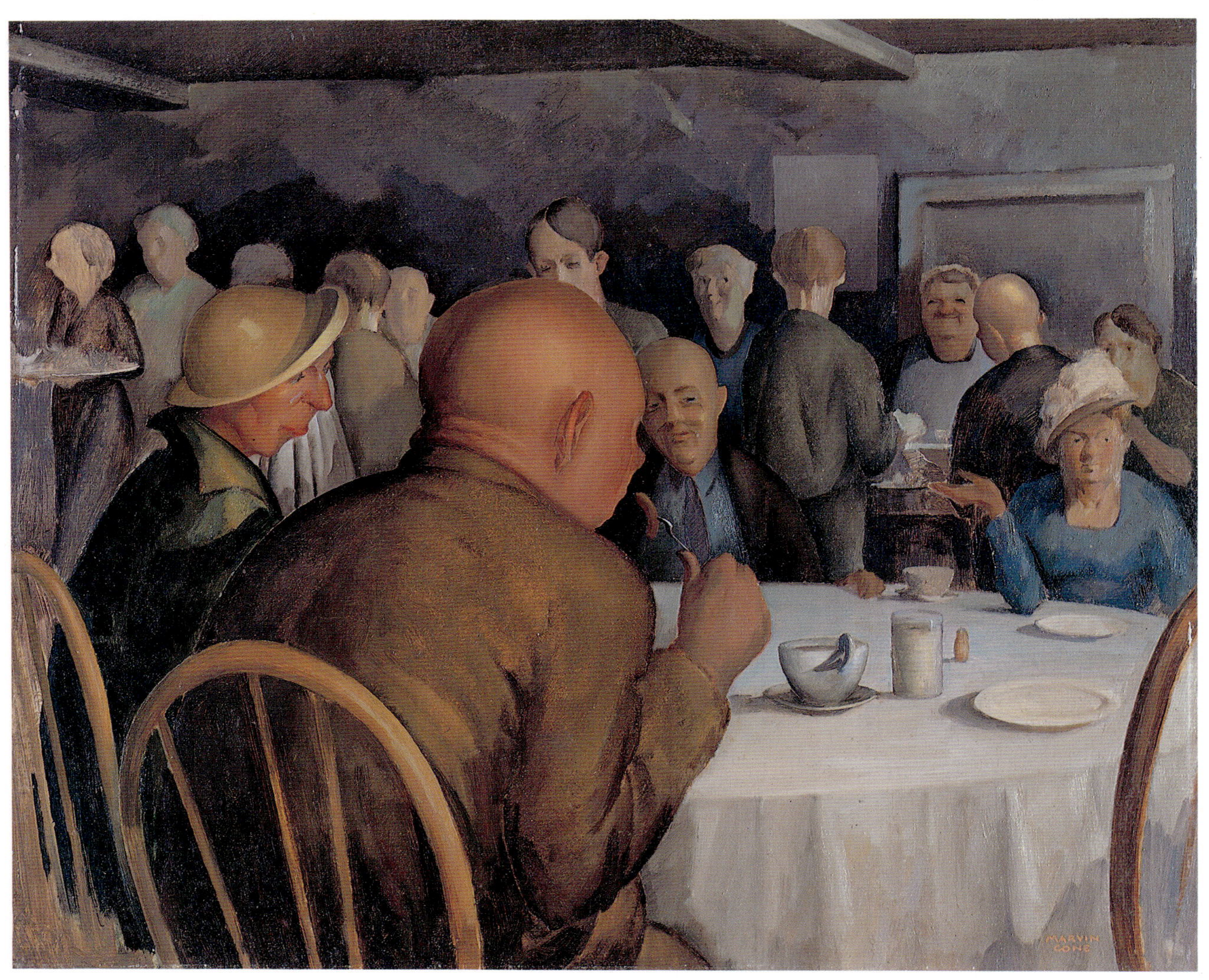


*Church Supper,* 1938–1939. Oil on composition board, 15″ x 18″. (Collection of Mr. and Mrs. John Bickel, Sr.)

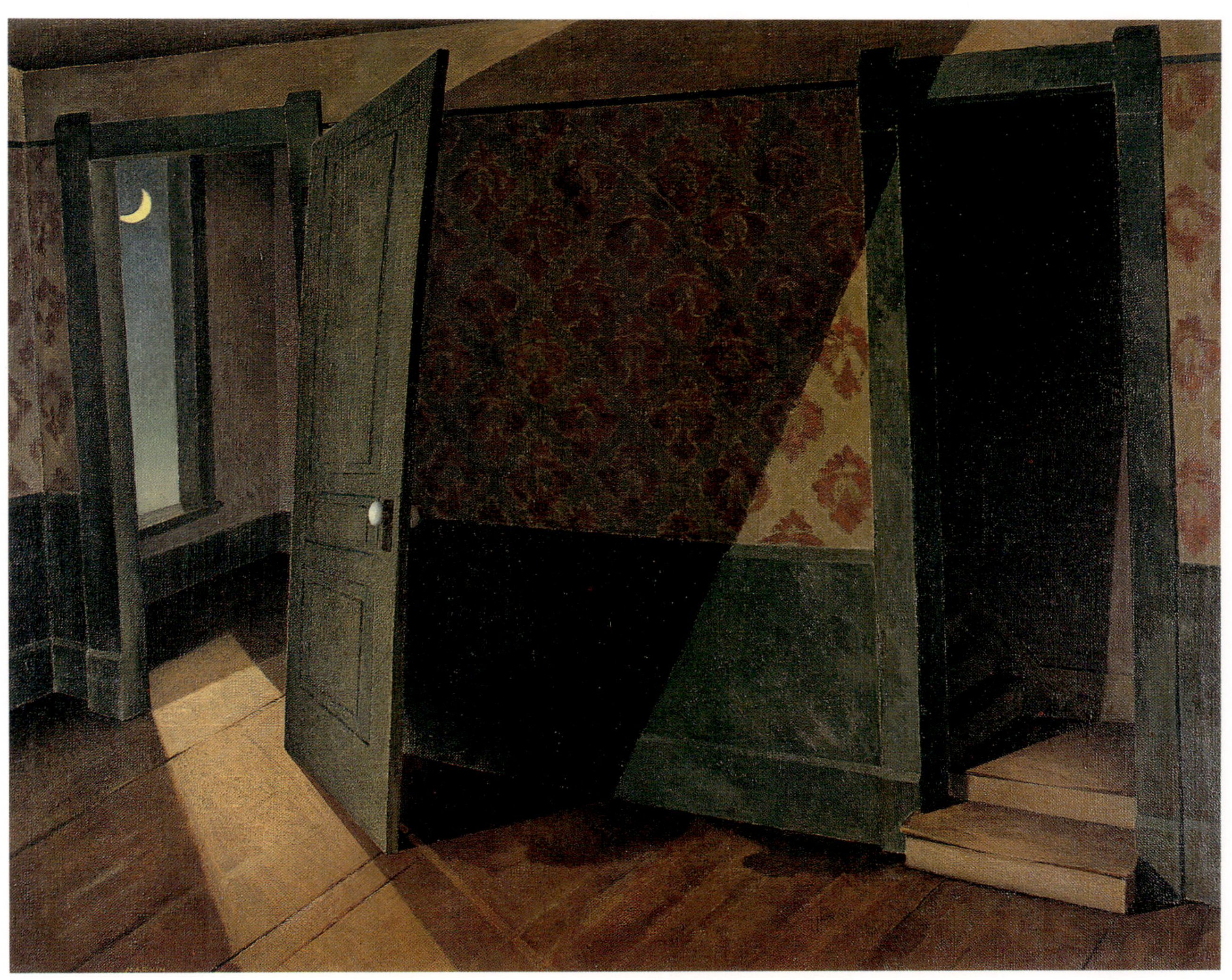

*Habitation,* 1939. Oil on canvas, 24″ x 30″. (Collection of Winnifred Cone)

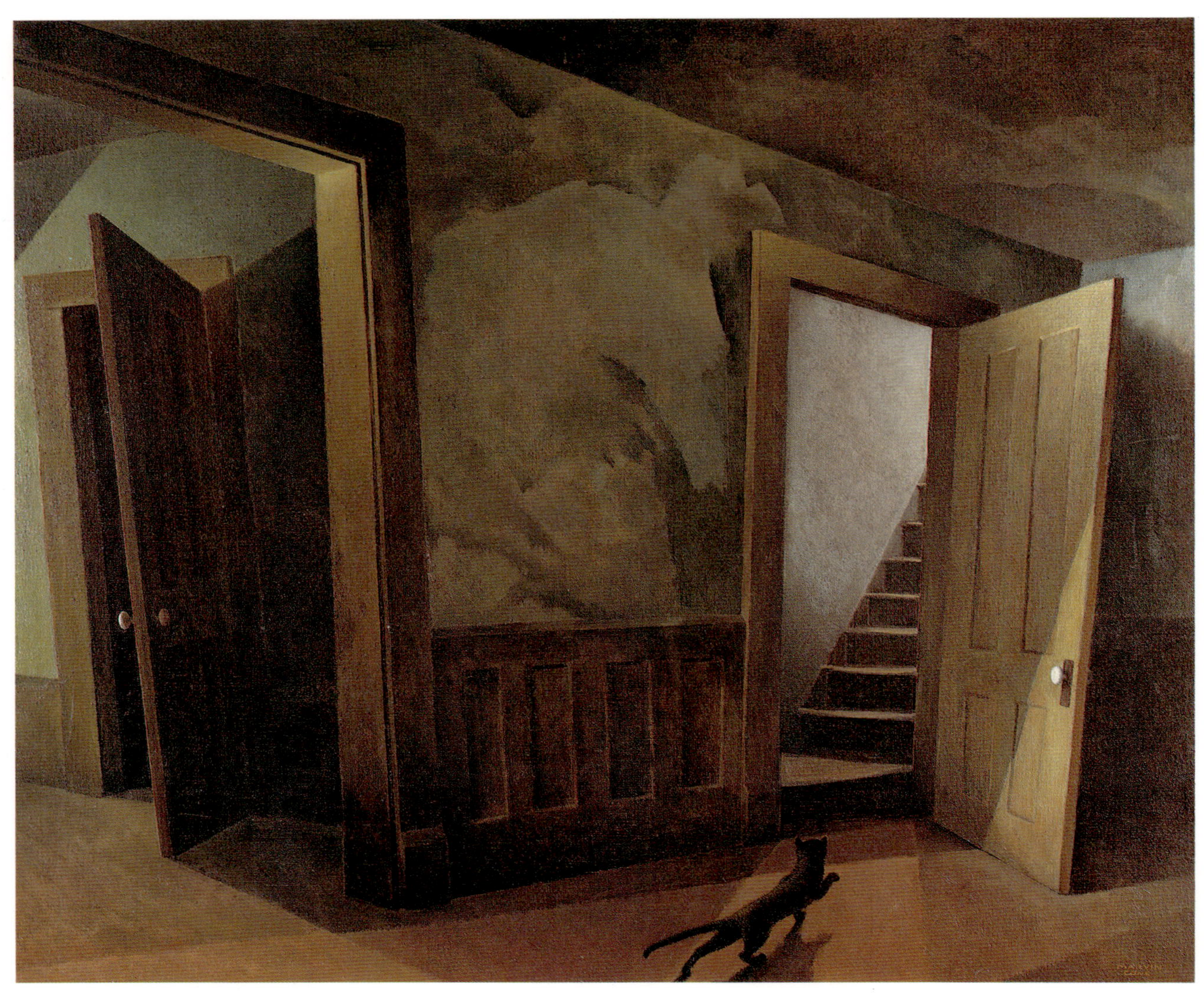

*Night Prowler,* 1939. Oil on canvas, 30″ x 36″. (Collection of Winnifred Cone)

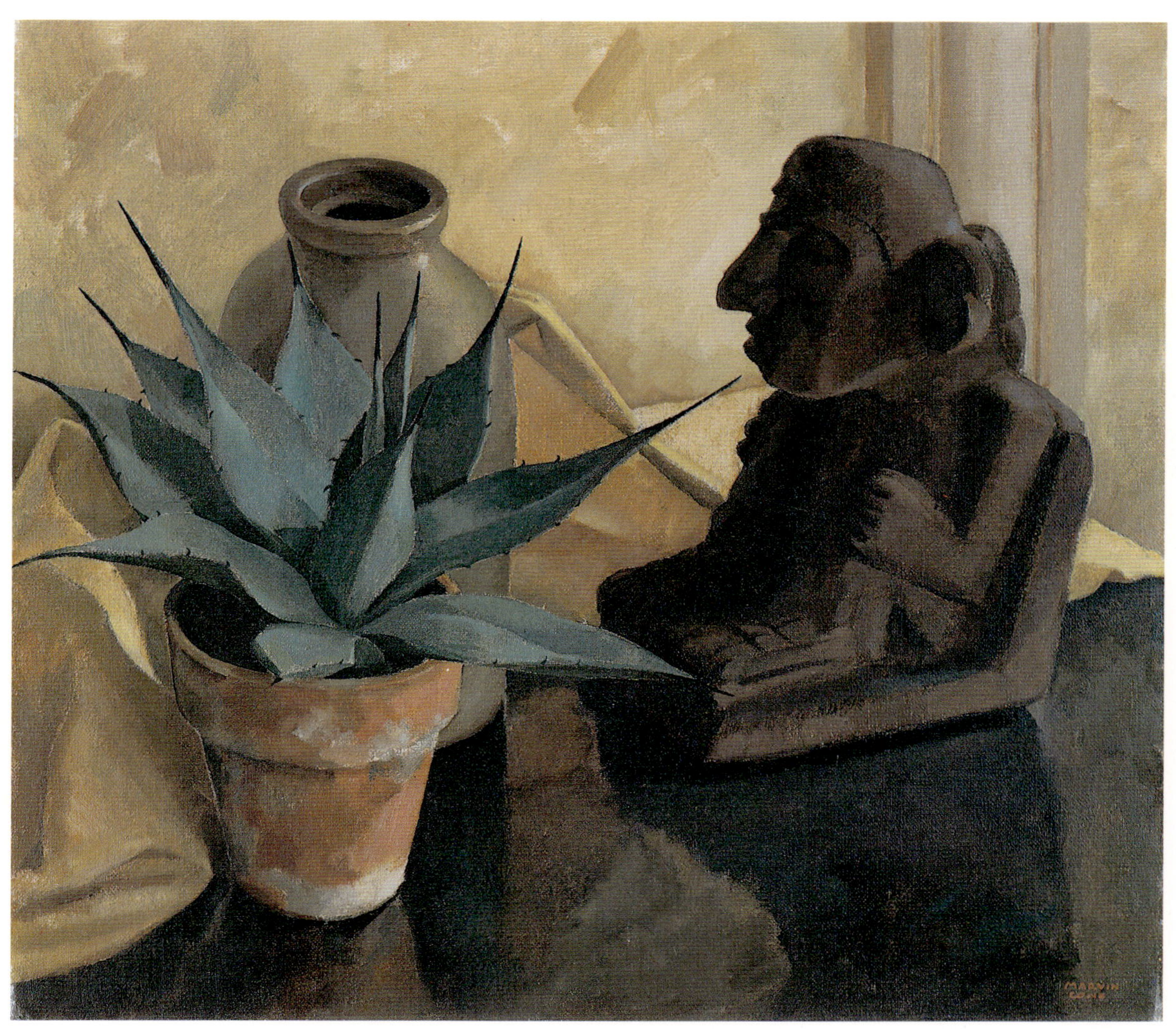


*Mexican Idol,* 1939. Oil on canvas, 19½″ x 21½″. (Collection of Mrs. Herbert S. Stamats)

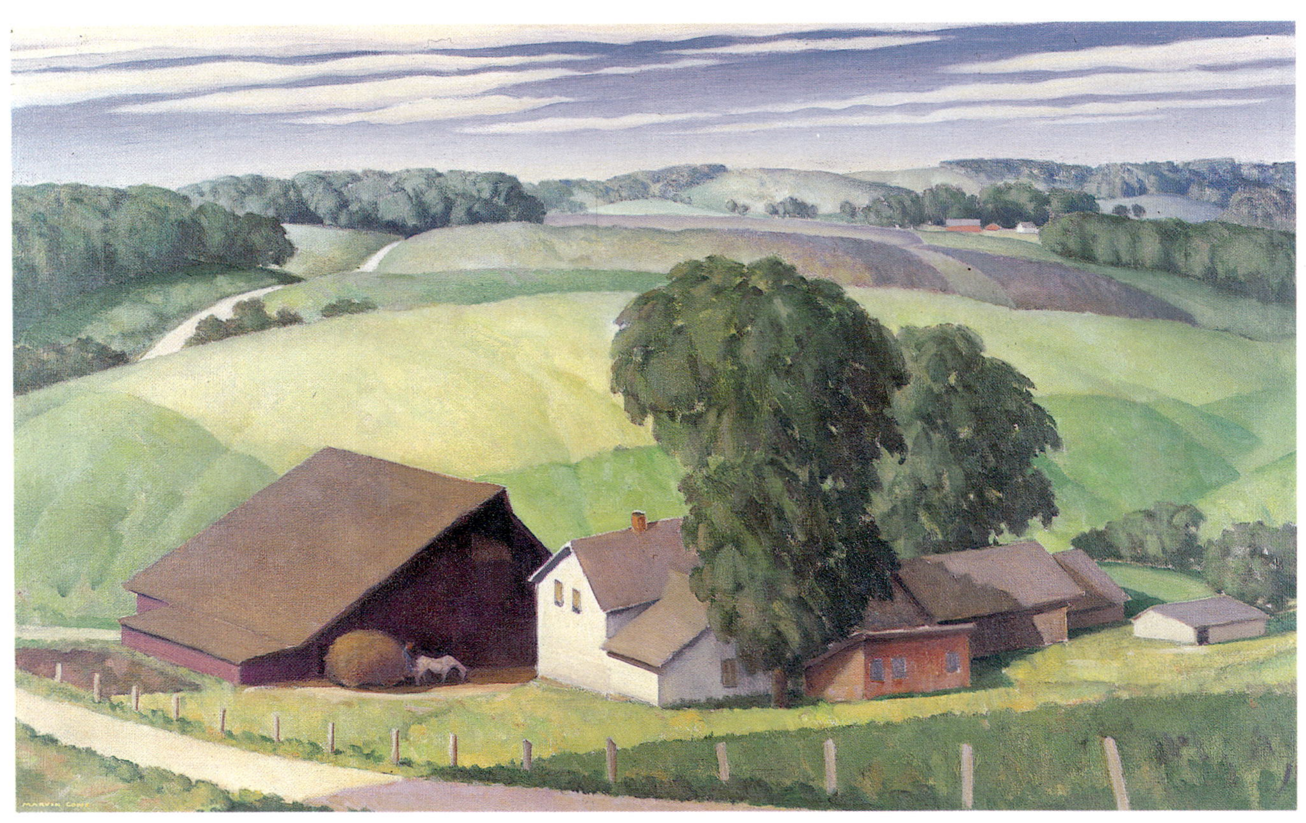

*Out Springville Way,* 1940. Oil on canvas, 16″ x 30″. (Collection of Mrs. Max Daehler)

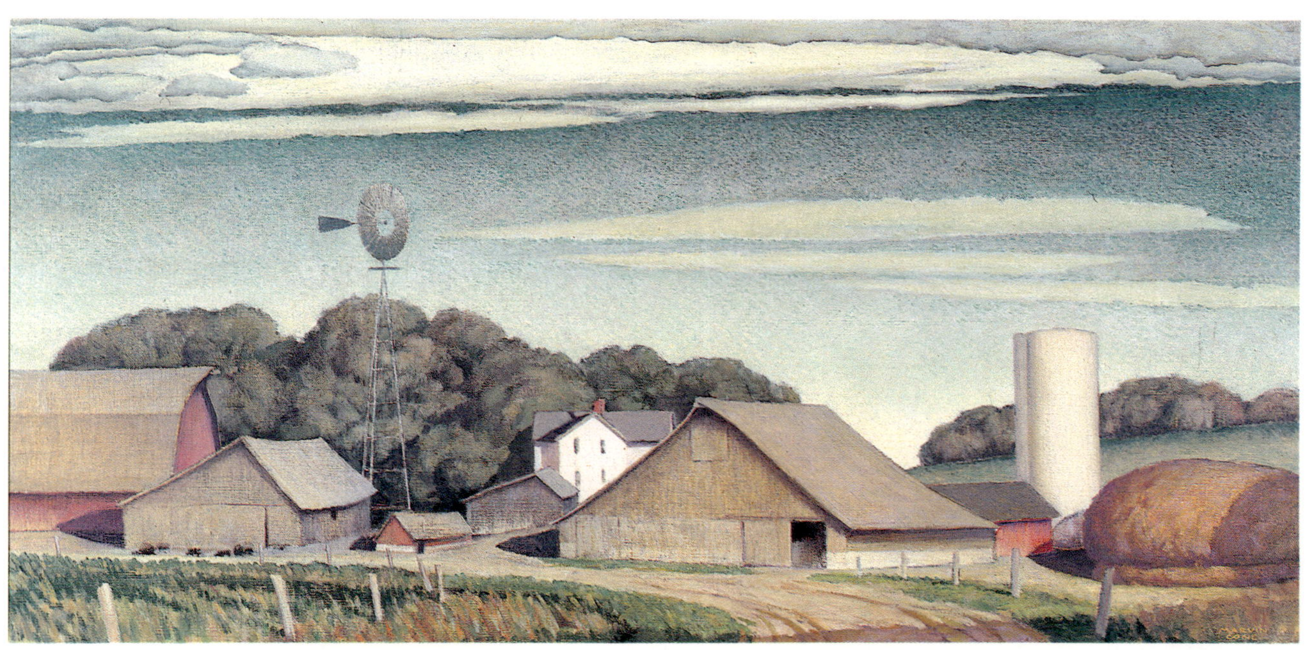

*From Iowa,* 1940. Oil on canvas, 16″ x 32″. (Cedar Rapids Museum of Art; Gift of Happy Young and John B. Turner II, 1983)

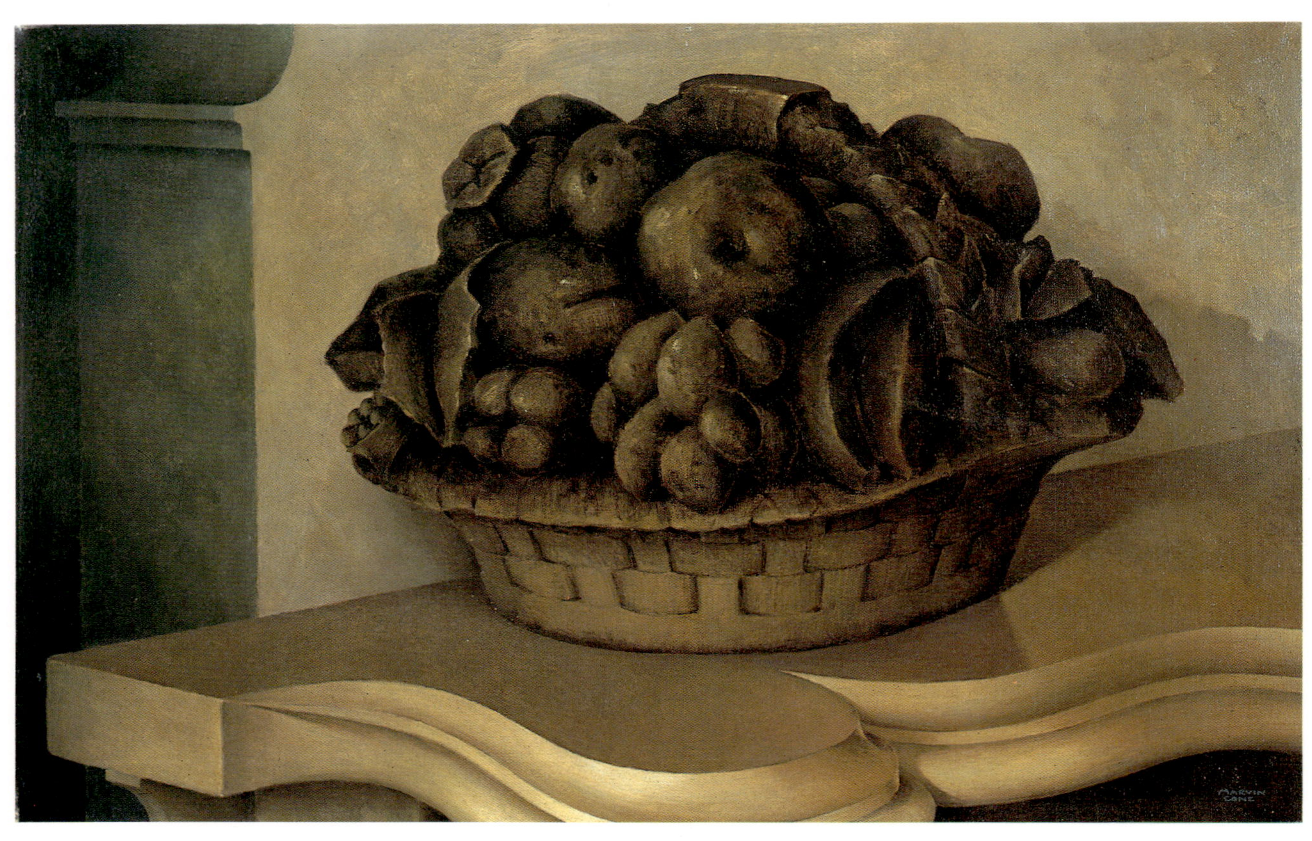

*Old Stone Carving,* c. 1940. Oil on canvas, 18″ x 28″. (Cedar Rapids Museum of Art; Gift of Happy Young and John B. Turner II, 1983)

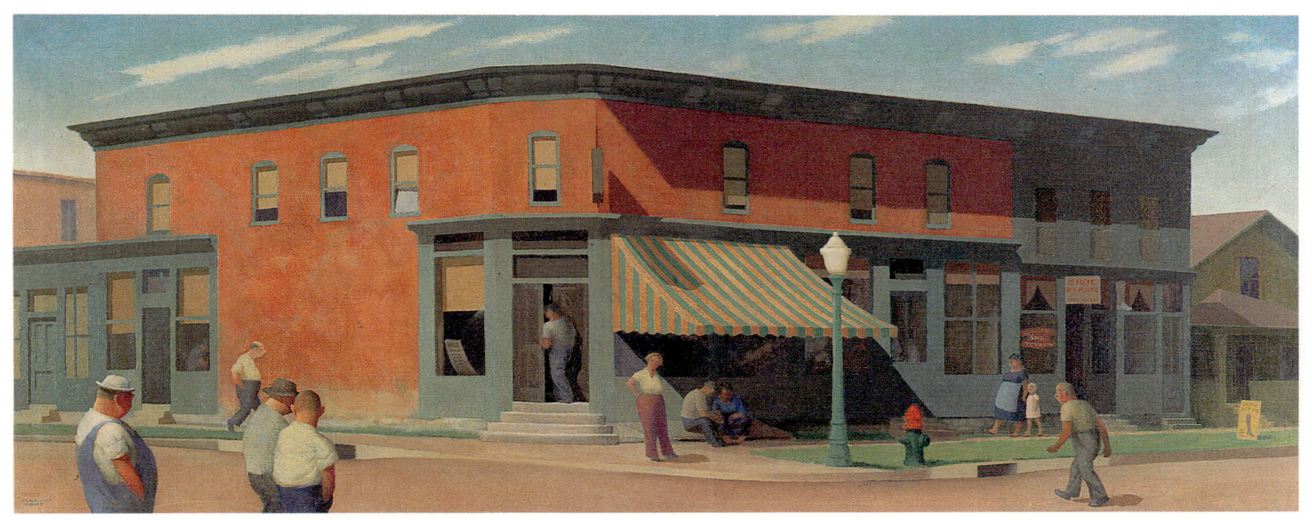

*Little Bohemia,* c. 1941. Oil on canvas, 16″ x 40″. (Coe College, Cedar Rapids)

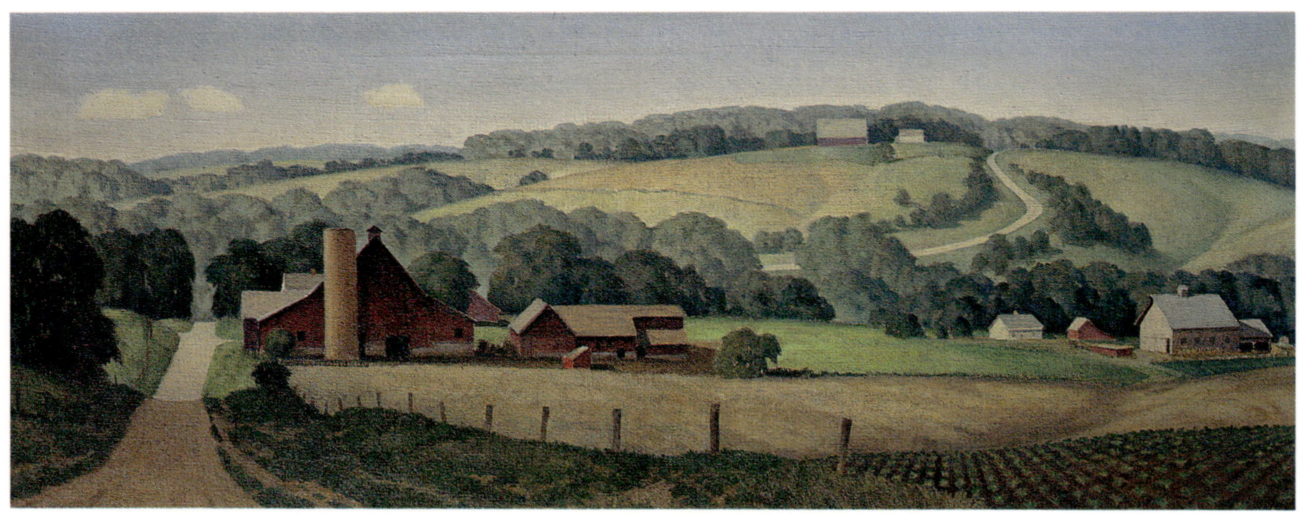

*Road to Waubeek*, 1941–1942. Oil on canvas, 15¾″ x 39½″. (Collection of Irving L. and Kathryn H. Churchill)

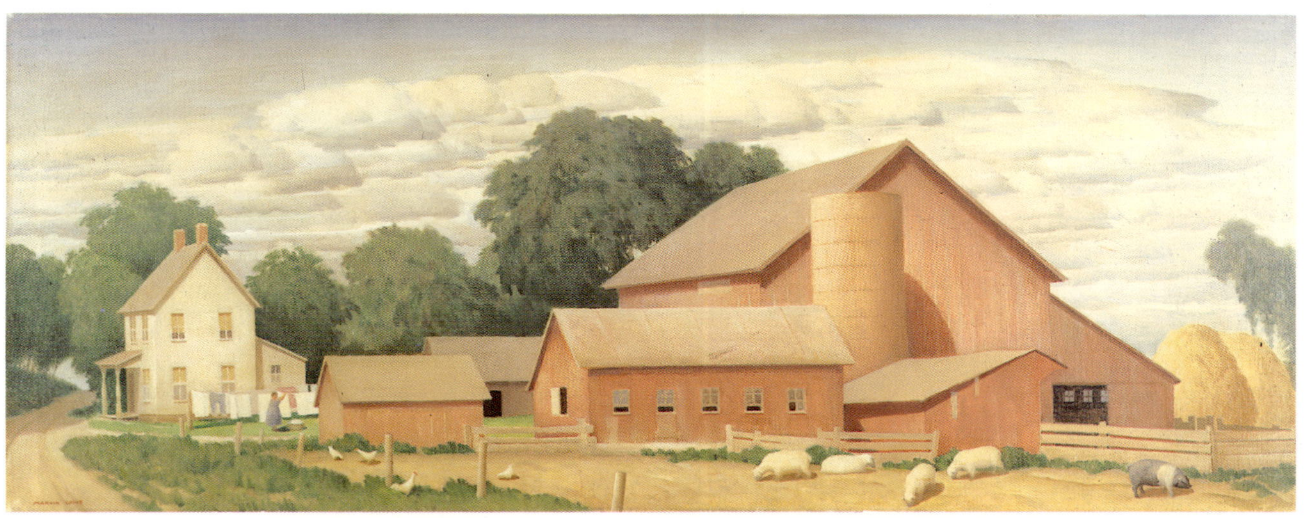

*Lafayette Farm,* 1942. Oil on canvas, 15⅞″ x 40″. (Cedar Rapids Museum of Art; Gift of Happy Young and John B. Turner II, 1983)

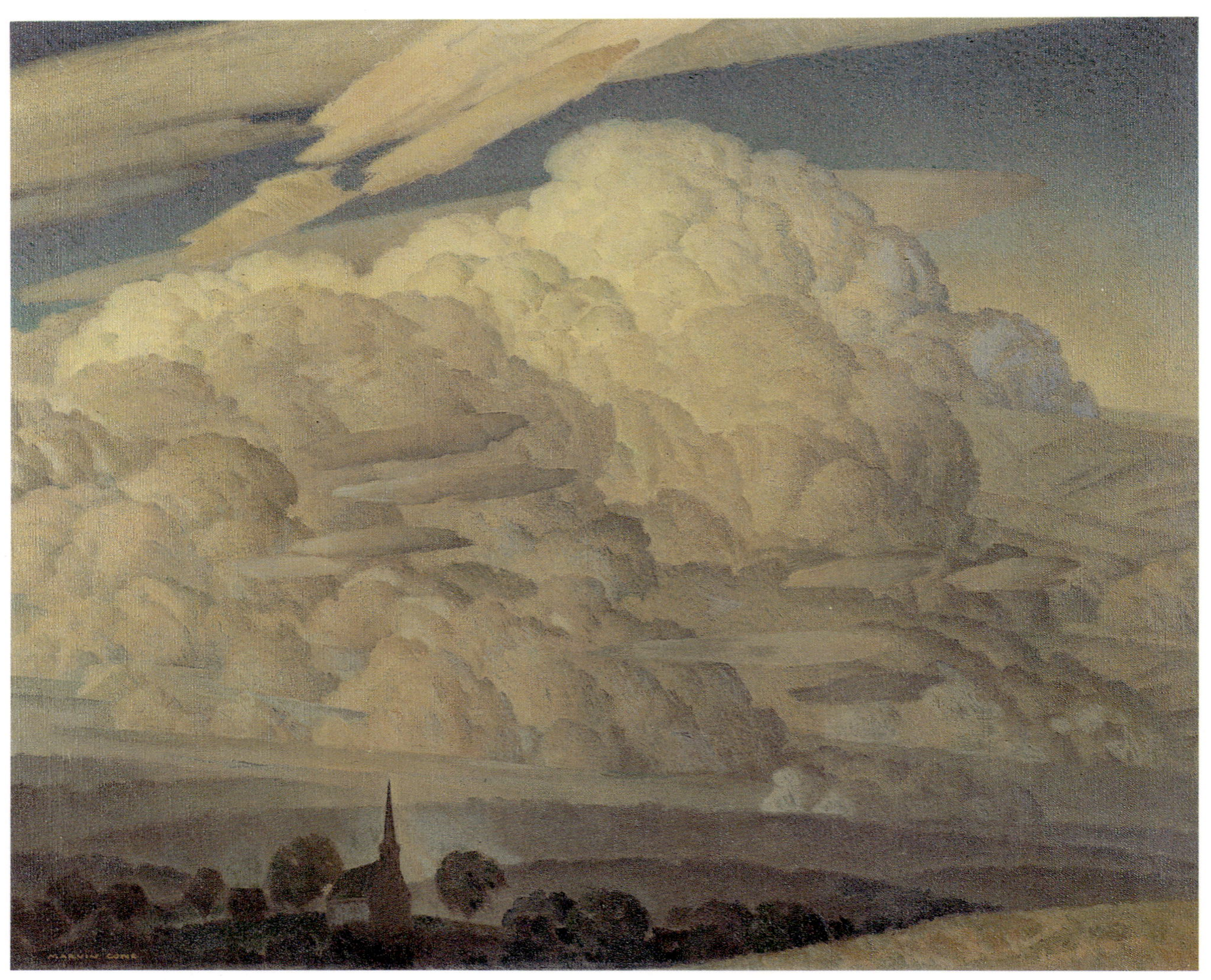

*Storm Clouds over Church,* c. 1943. Oil on canvas, 24″ x 30″. (Private collection)

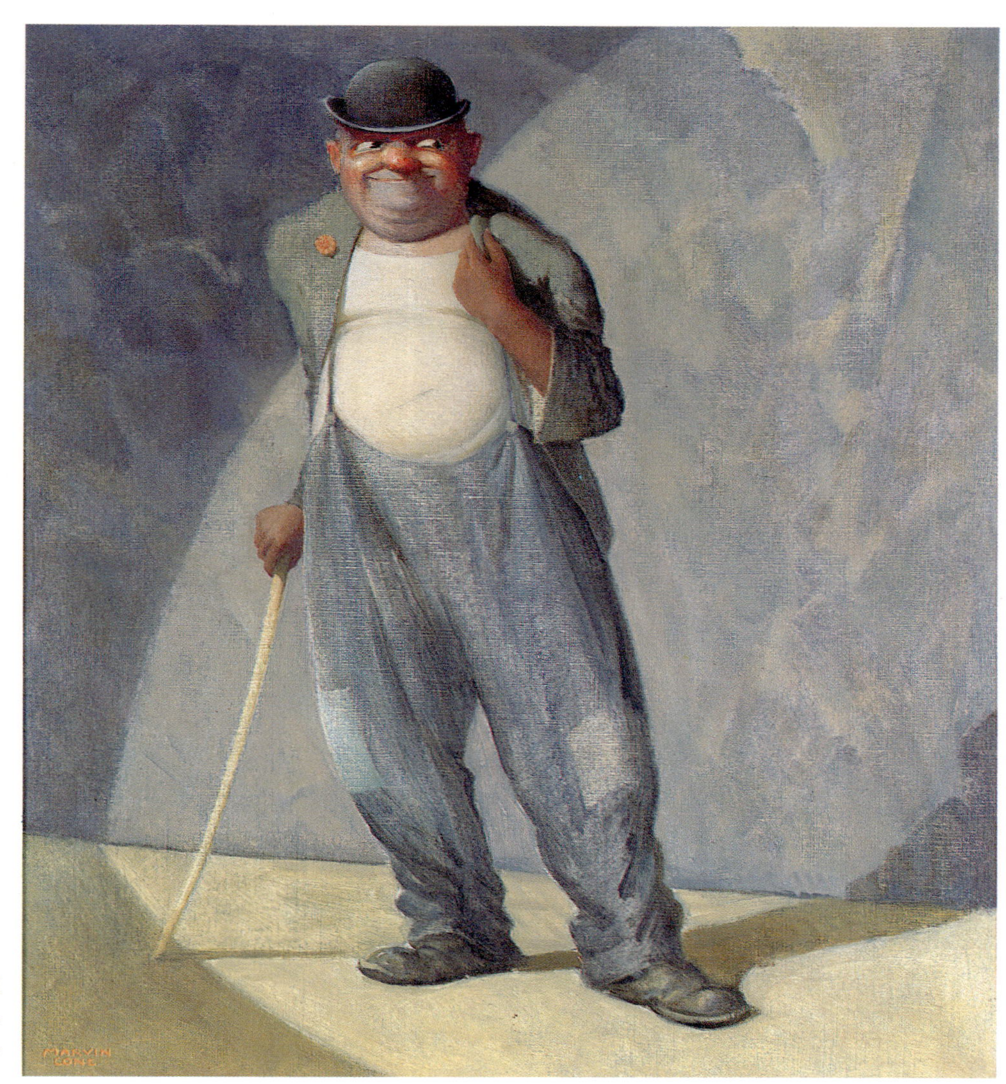

*Tramp Comedian,* 1945. Oil on canvas board, 19½″ x 18″. (Collection of Peter O. Stamats)

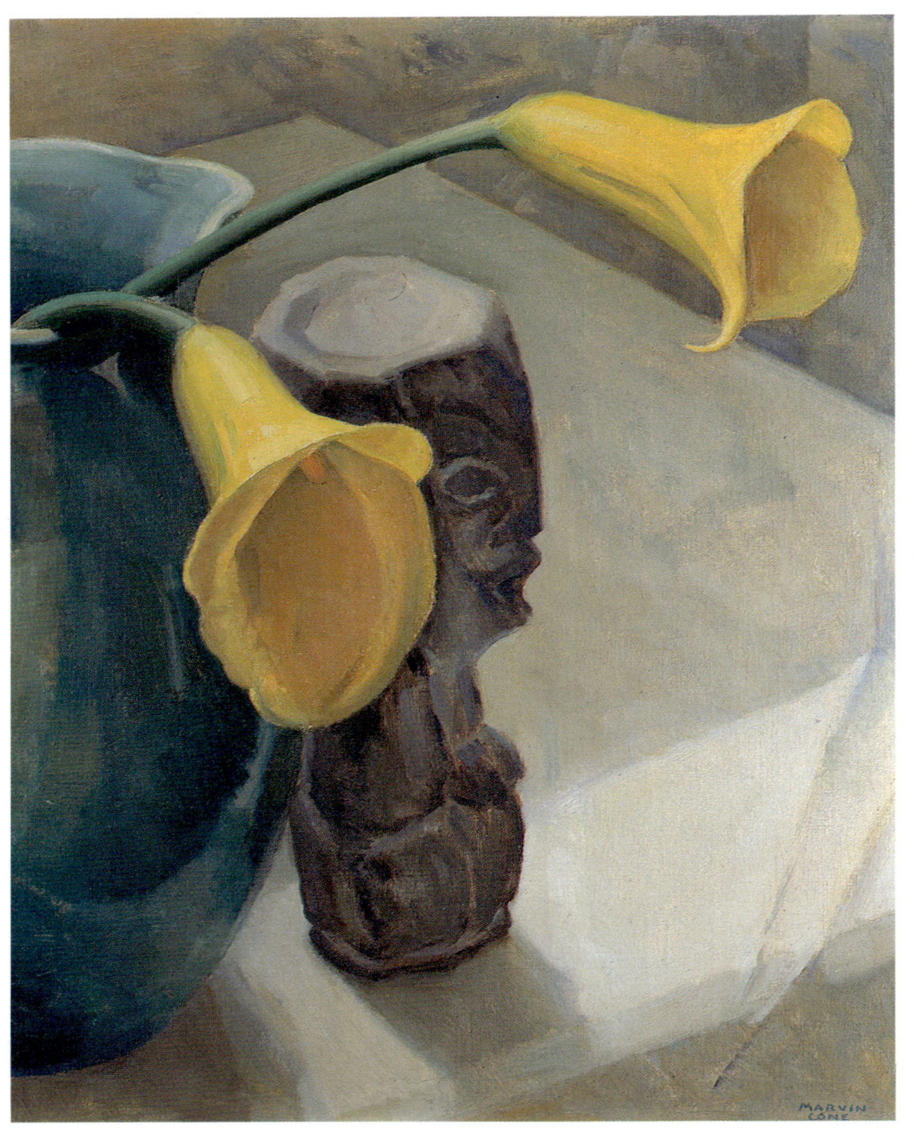


*Lilies for a God*, 1945. Oil on canvas board, 18″ x 15″. (Coe College, Cedar Rapids; Gift of Mr. and Mrs. William P. Whipple)

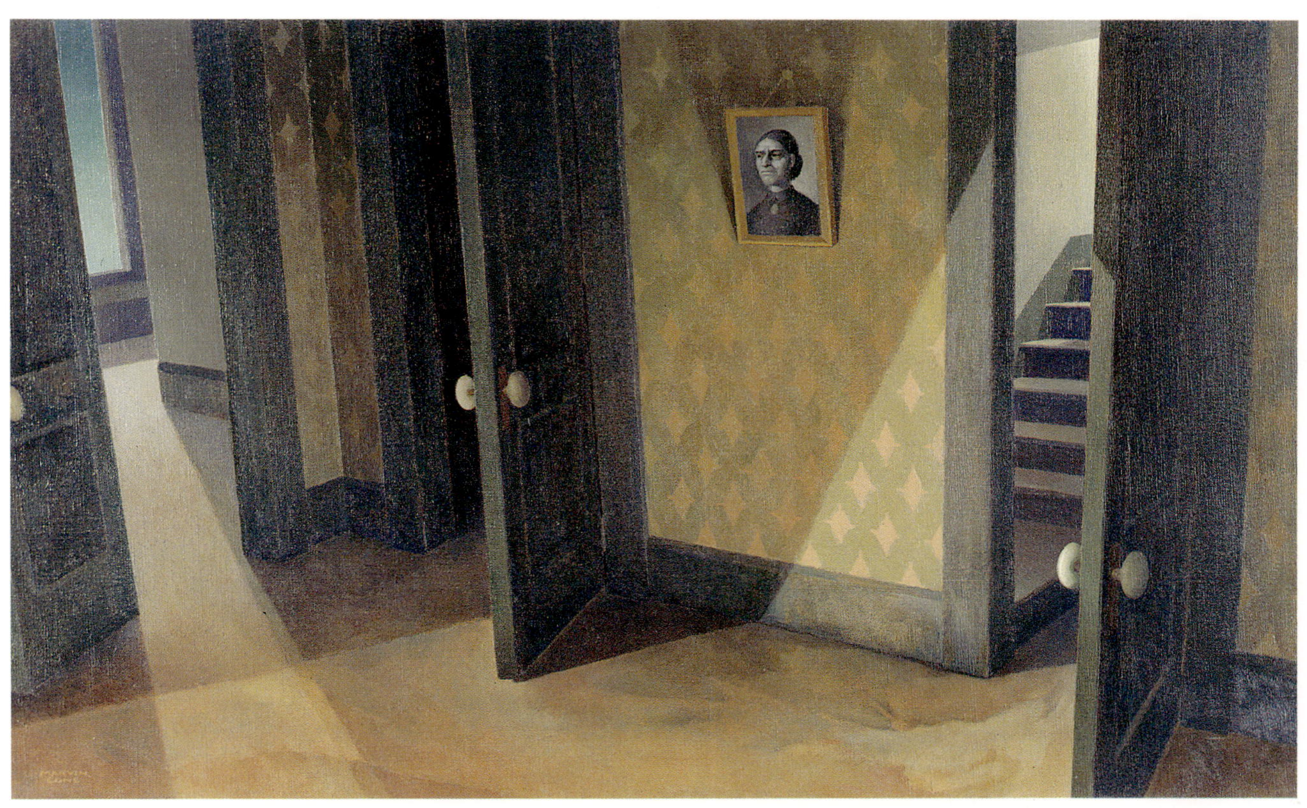

*Dear Departed*, 1946. Oil on canvas, 18″ x 30″. (Cedar Rapids Museum of Art; Gift of Winnifred Cone and Family, 1980)

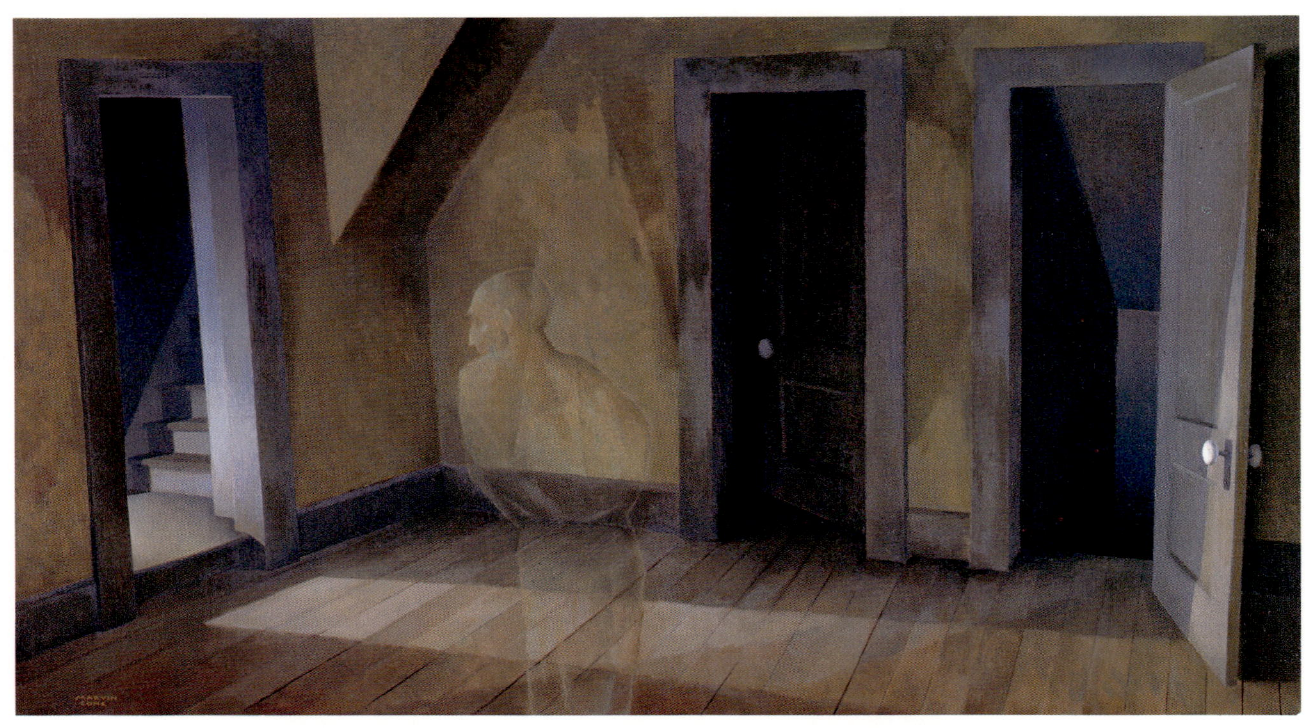

*This Was Doubtless He,* 1946. Oil on canvas, 19¾″ x 34⅞″. (Cedar Rapids Museum of Art; Gift of Winnifred Cone and Family, and Museum Purchase, 1983)

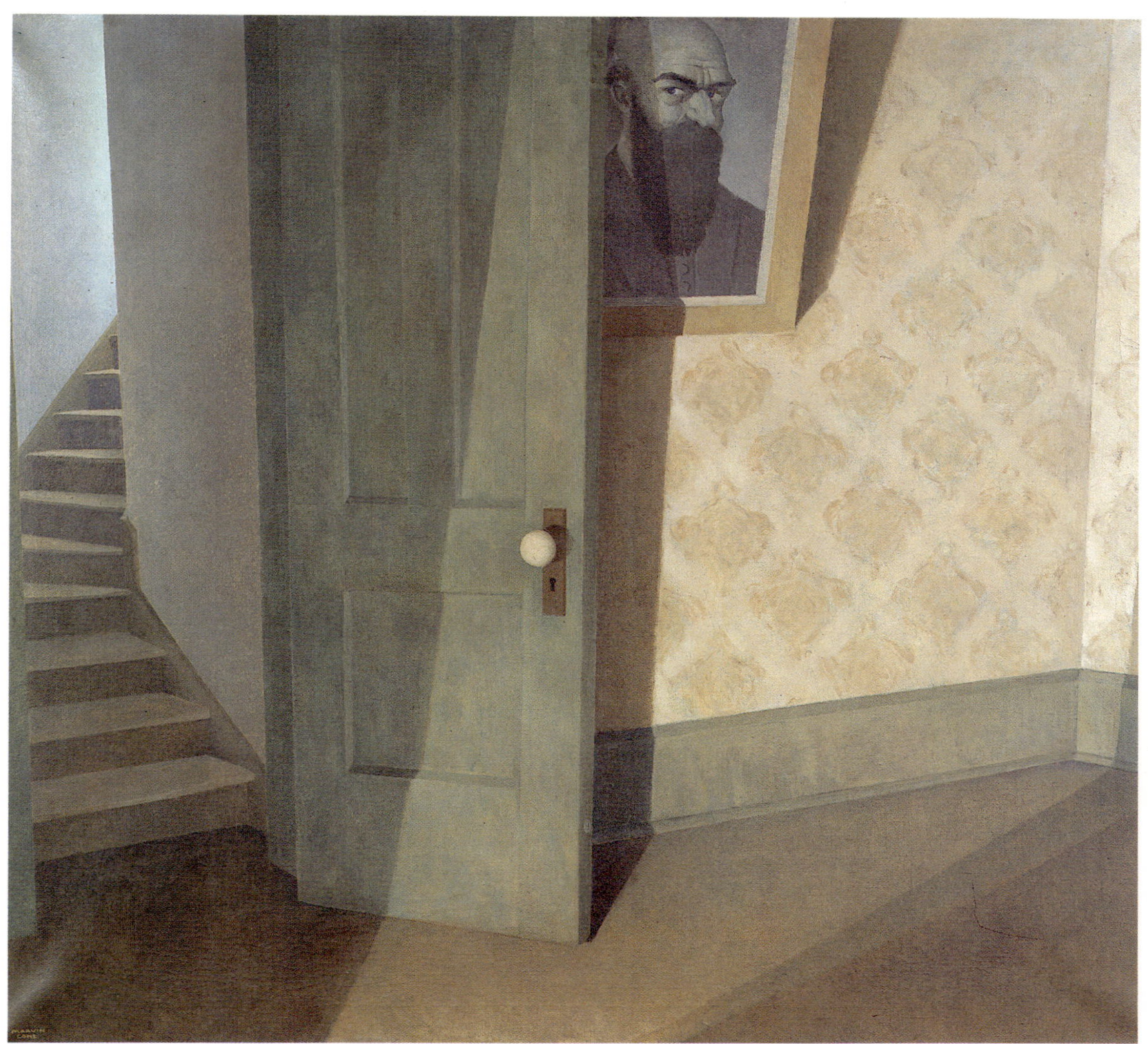

*There's Uncle Ben Again,* c. 1947. Oil on canvas, 36″ x 40″. (Private collection)

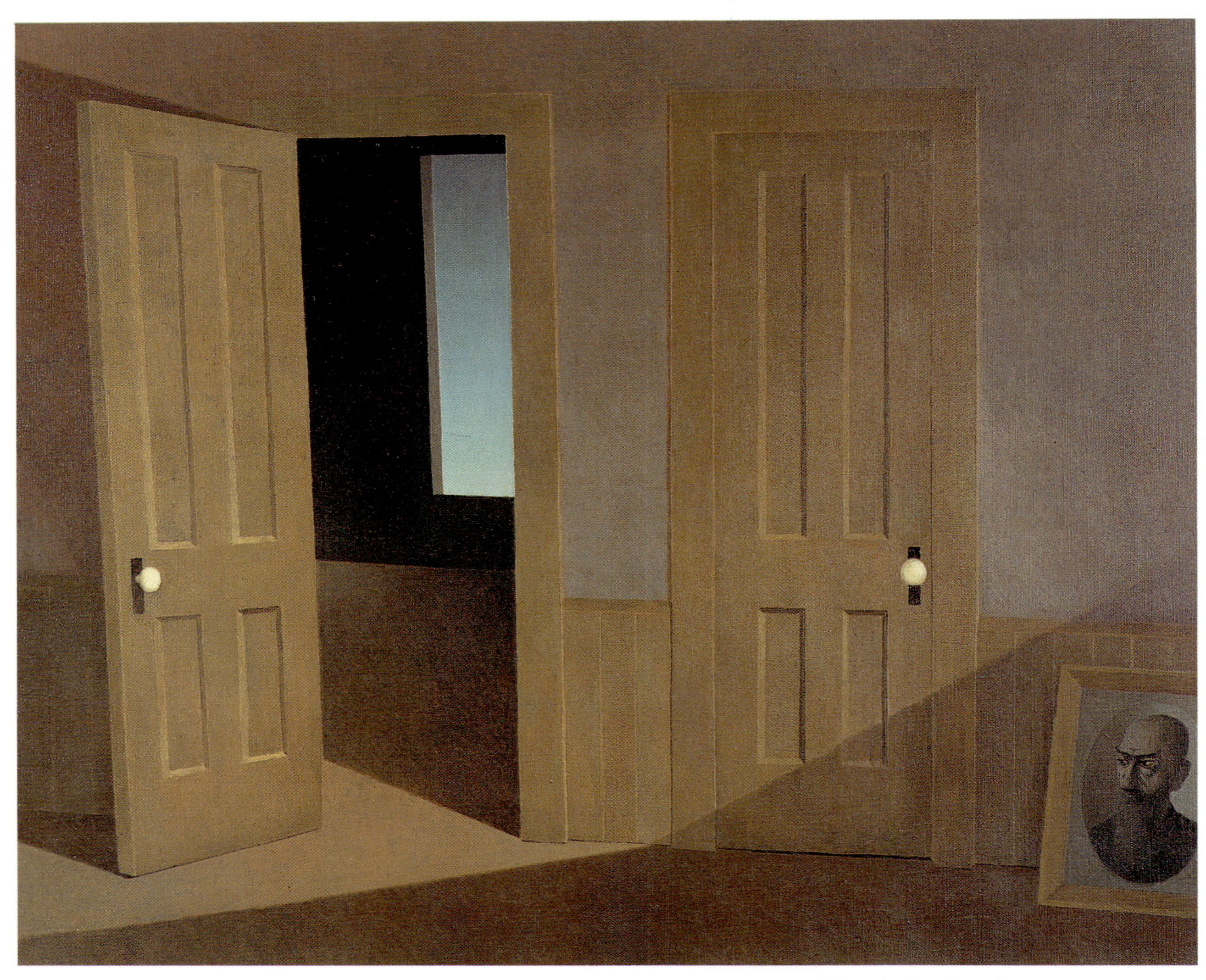

*Room with Uncle Ben,* c. 1947–1948. Oil on canvas, 24″ x 30″. (Cedar Rapids Museum of Art; Gift of Winnifred Cone and Family, and Museum Purchase, 1983)

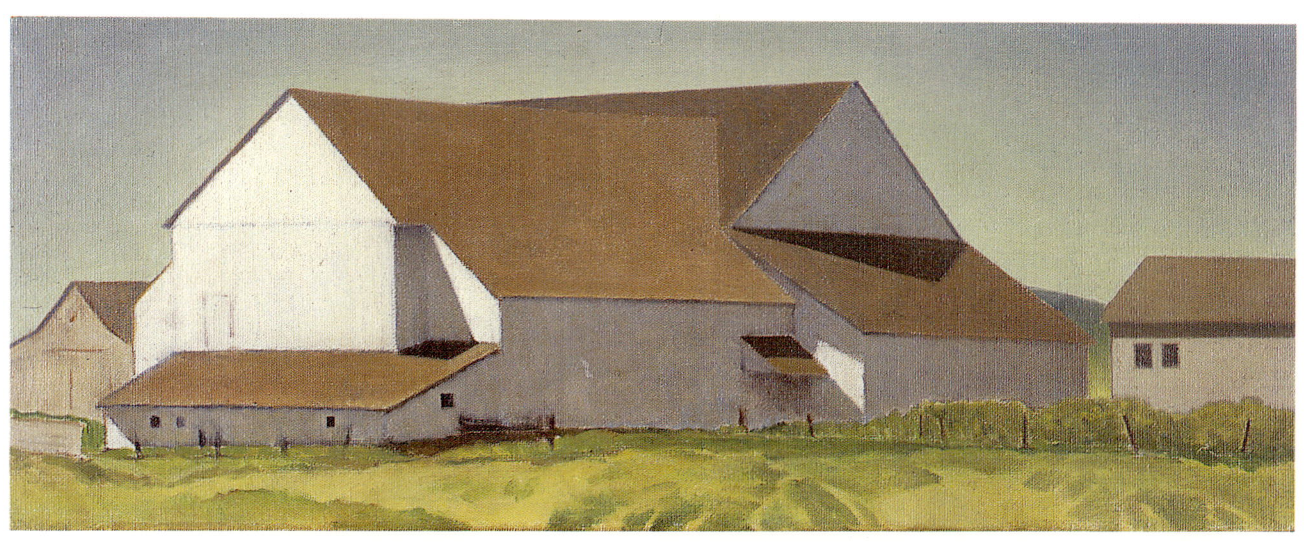

*White Pennsylvania Barn,* 1948. Oil on canvas, 9″ x 22″. (Private collection)

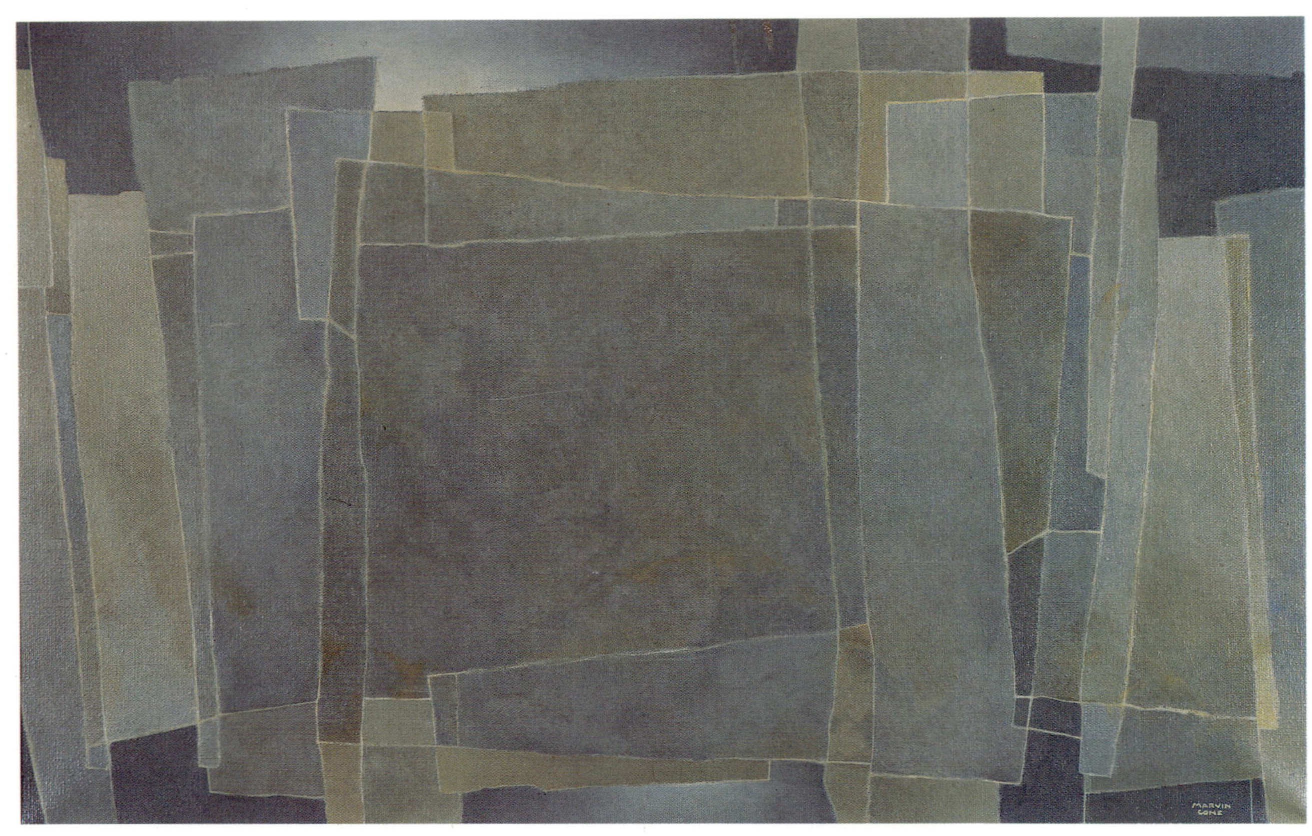


*Inner Light,* 1950. Oil on canvas, 18¼″ x 28″. (Cedar Rapids Museum of Art; Gift in Memory of Arthur Poe, 1951)

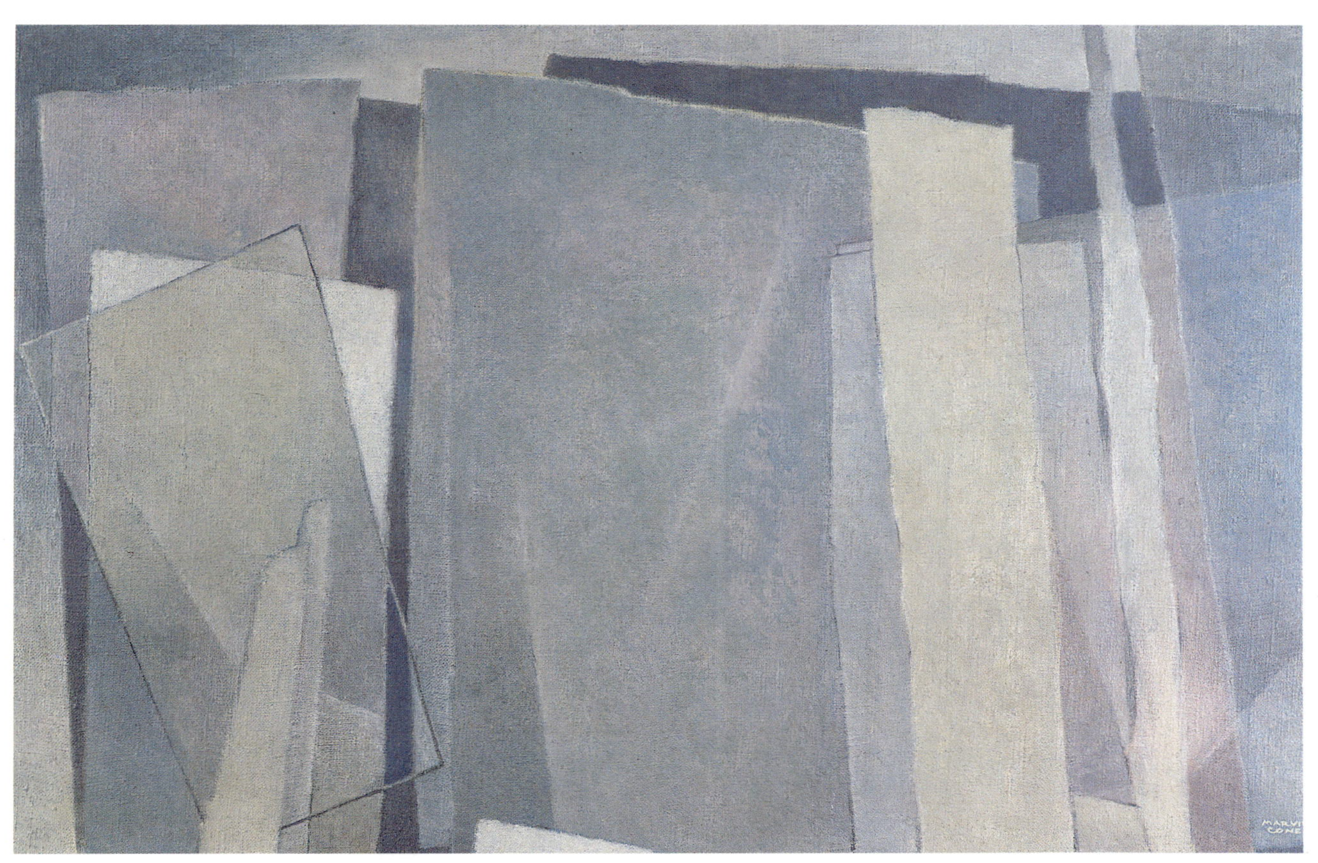

*Memorial,* 1950. Oil on canvas, 16″ x 24″. (Collection of Winnifred Cone)

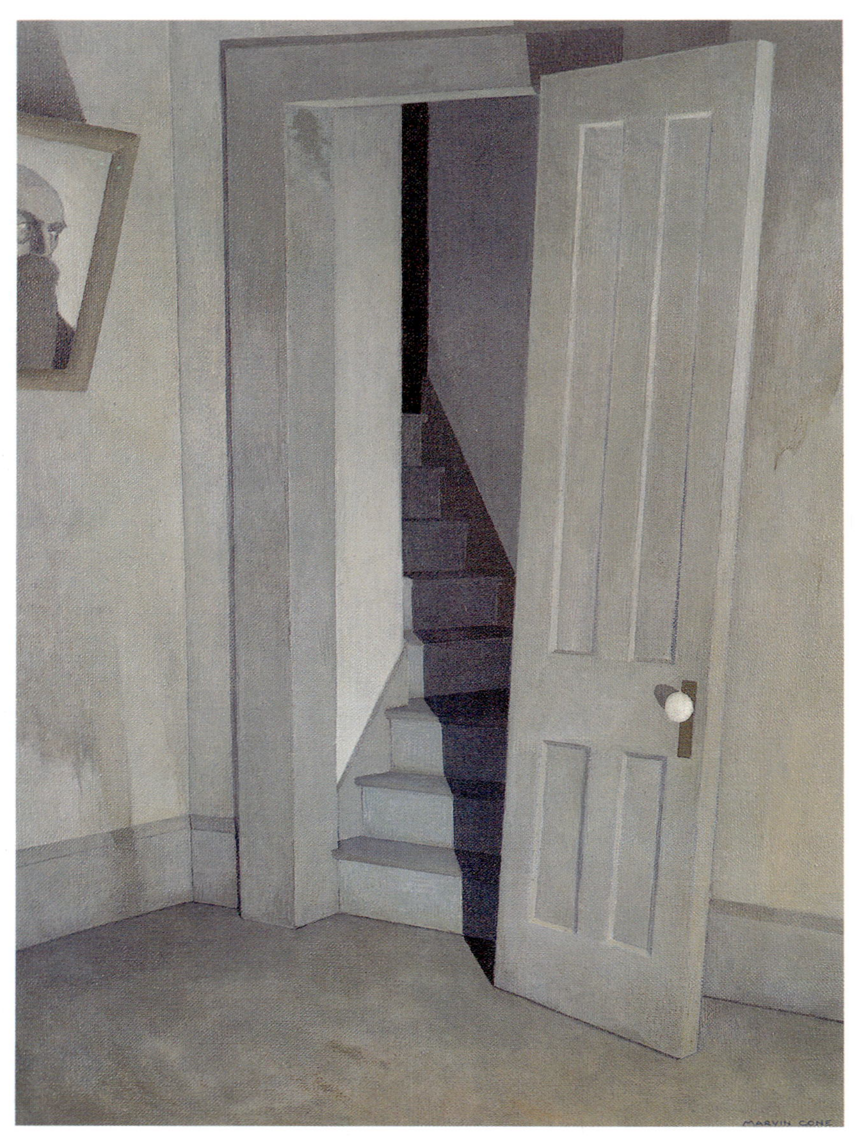


*Blue Stairs,* 1951. Oil on canvas, 18″ x 24″. (Private collection)

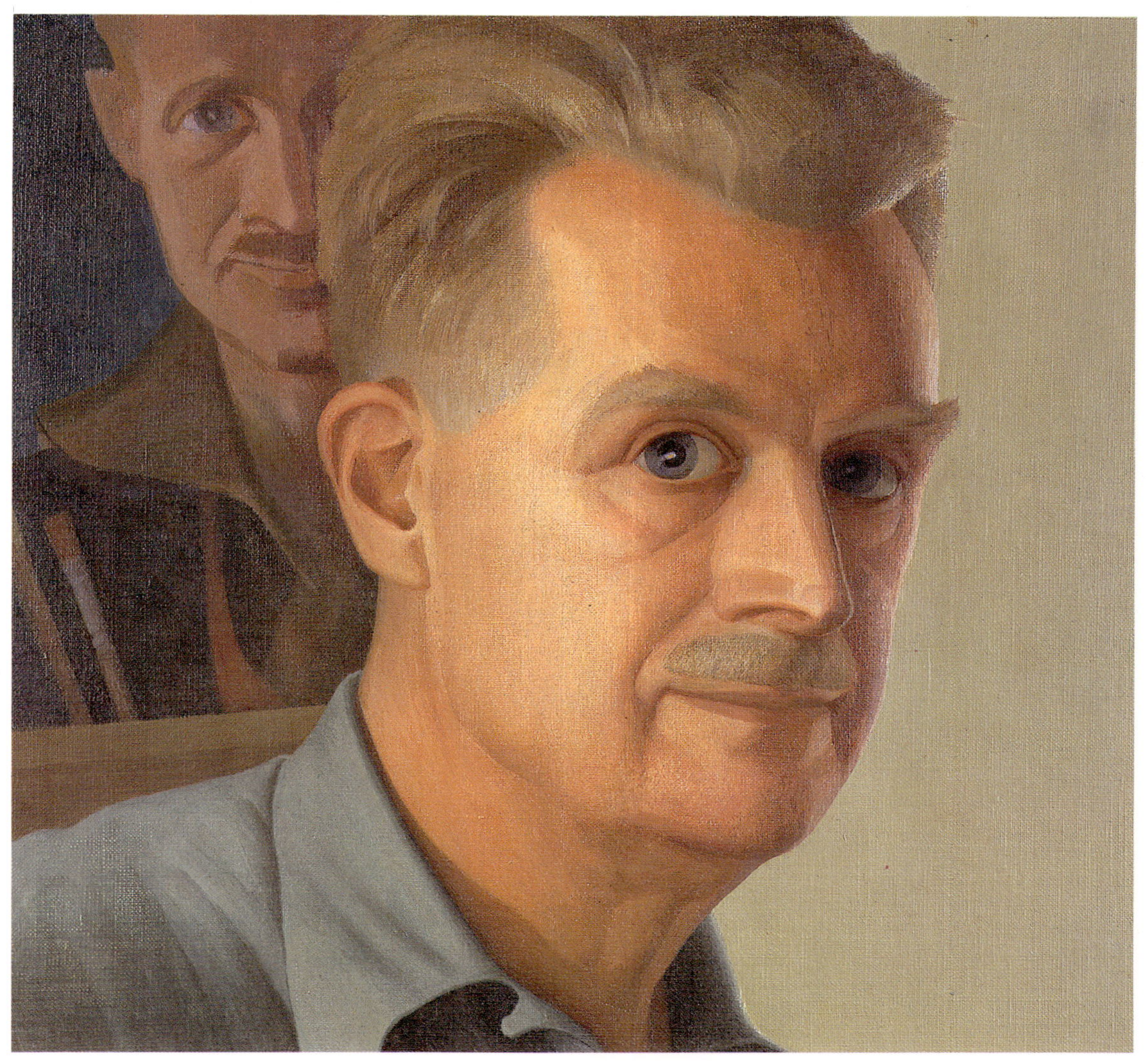

*Self-Portrait—with Malnutrition,* c. 1955. Oil on masonite, 14¾" x 16¾". (Collection of Winnifred Cone)

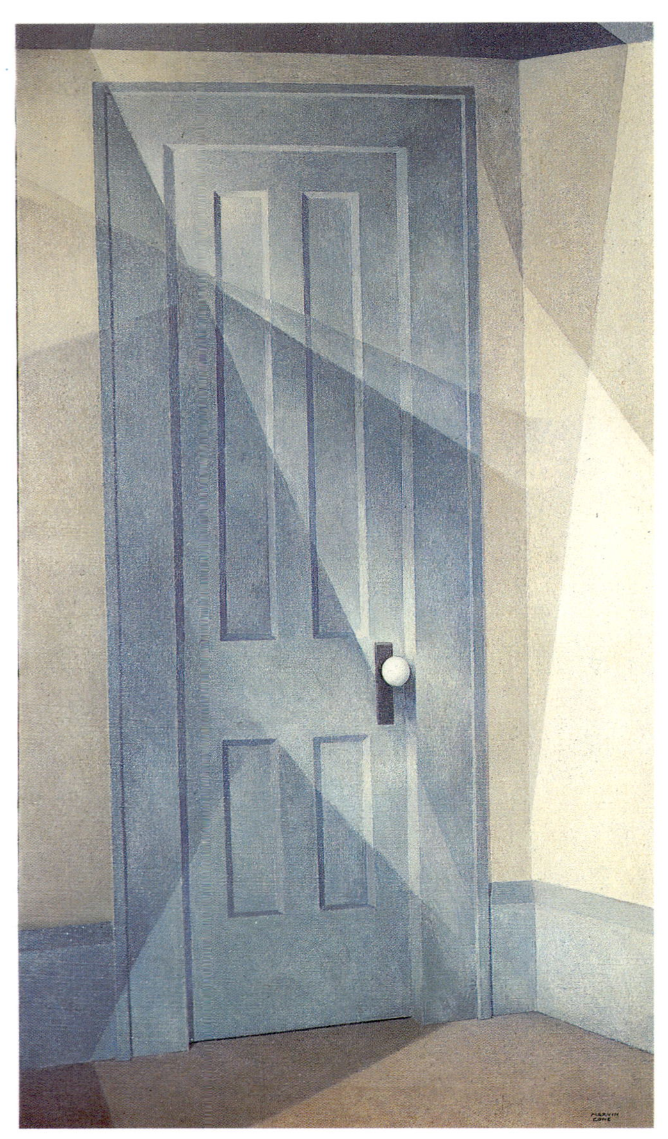

*This Was the Door,* 1956. Oil on canvas, 36″ x 20″. (Collection of Mr. and Mrs. Fred C. Fisher)

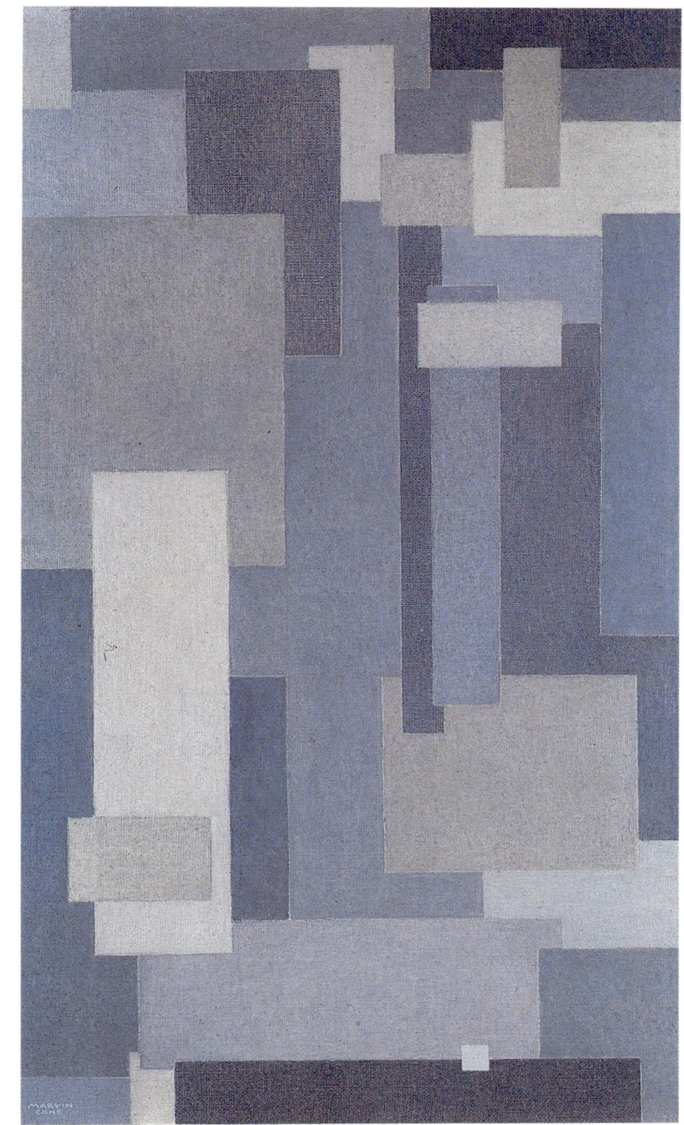


*Pattern of Rectangles,* 1957. Oil on canvas, 30″ x 18″. (Cedar Rapids Museum of Art; Gift of Winnifred Cone and Family, and Museum Purchase, 1983)

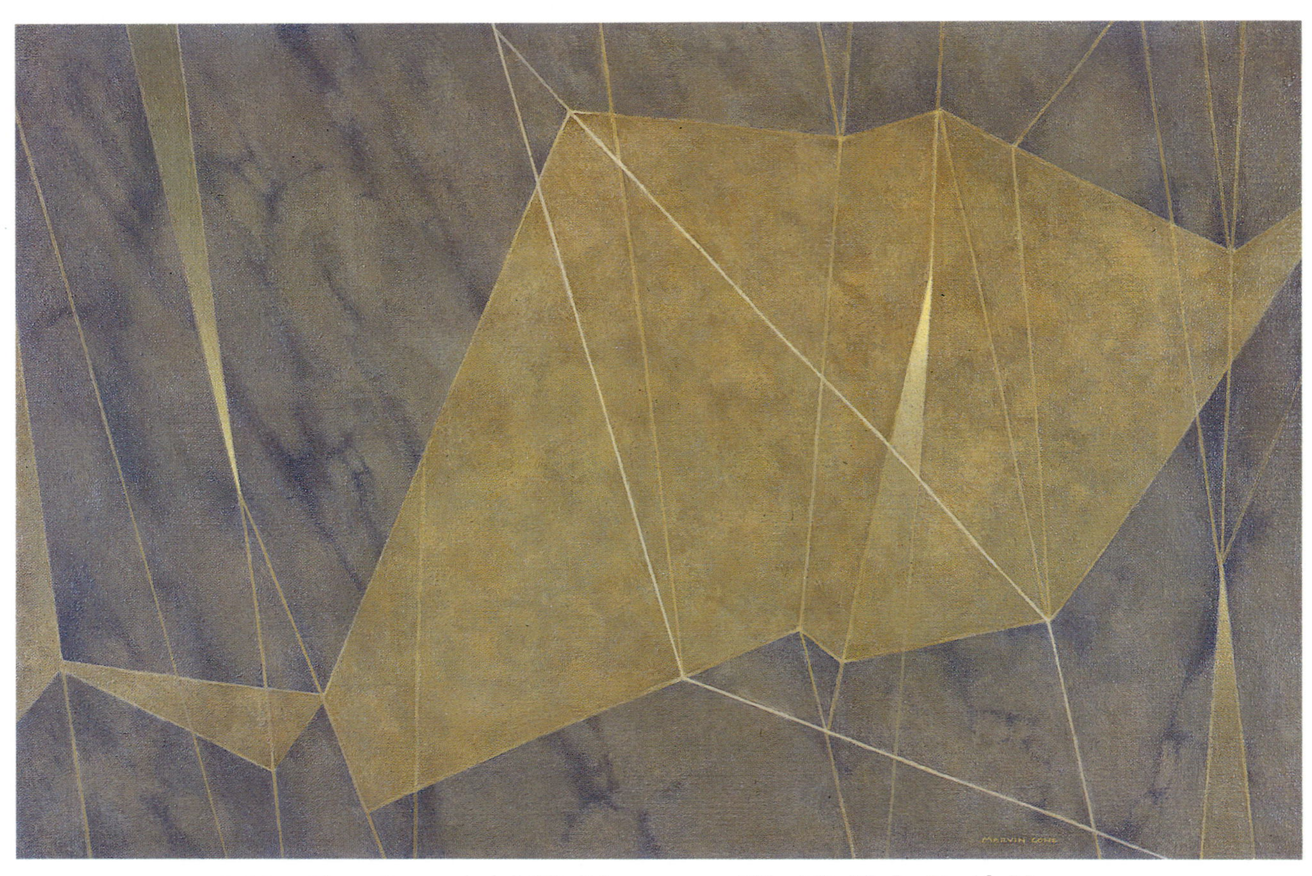

*Golden Object Suspended,* 1959. Oil on canvas, 20″ x 30″. (Cedar Rapids Museum of Art; Gift of John S. Vavra In Memory of Adeline J. Vavra, 1983)

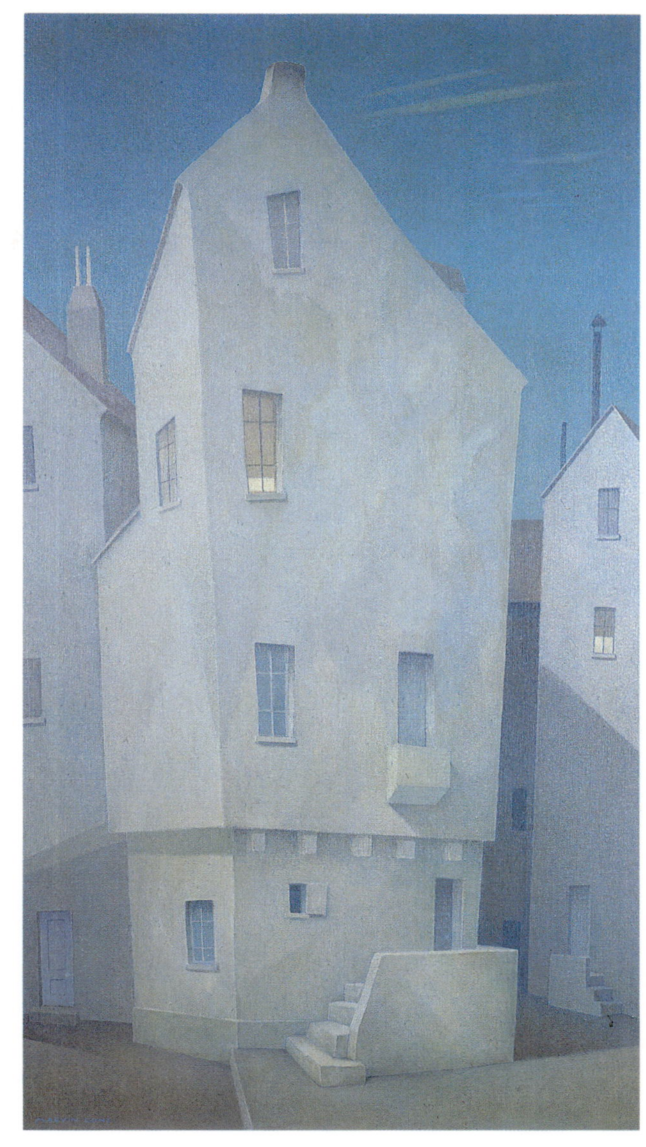

*A House That Jack Built,* 1960. Oil on canvas, 36″ x 20″. (Collection of Mr. and Mrs. Arthur A. Collins)

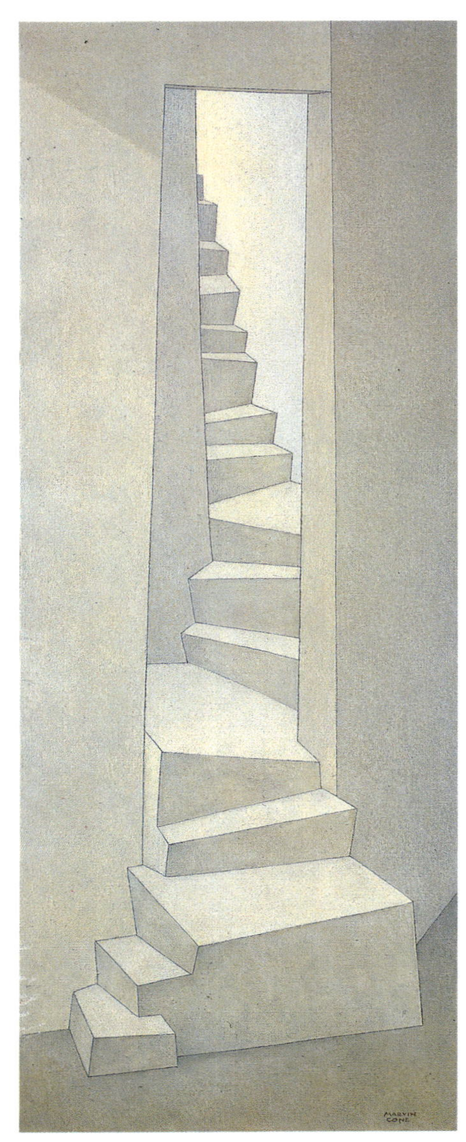


*Rakish Steps*, 1961. Oil on canvas, 36″ x 14″. (Cedar Rapids Museum of Art; Gift of Winnifred Cone and Family, and Museum Purchase, 1982)

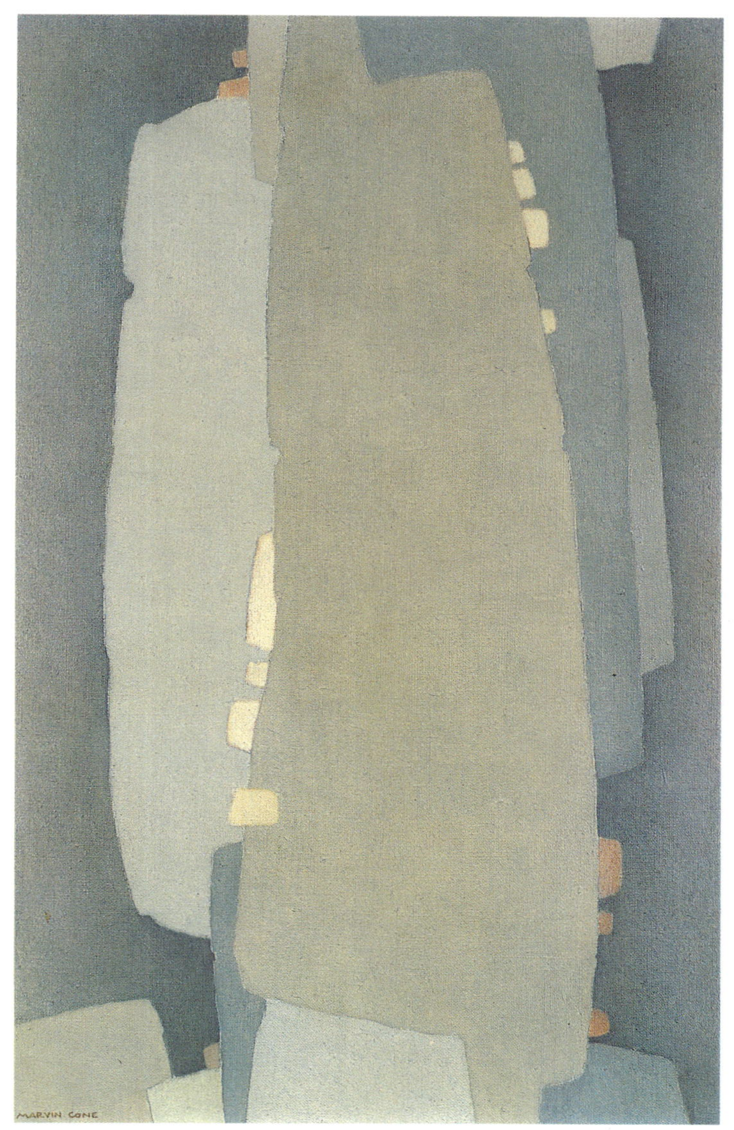


*Enigma*, 1961. Oil on canvas, 23⅞″ x 15⅞″. (Cedar Rapids Museum of Art; Gift of Winnifred Cone and Family, and Museum Purchase, 1982)

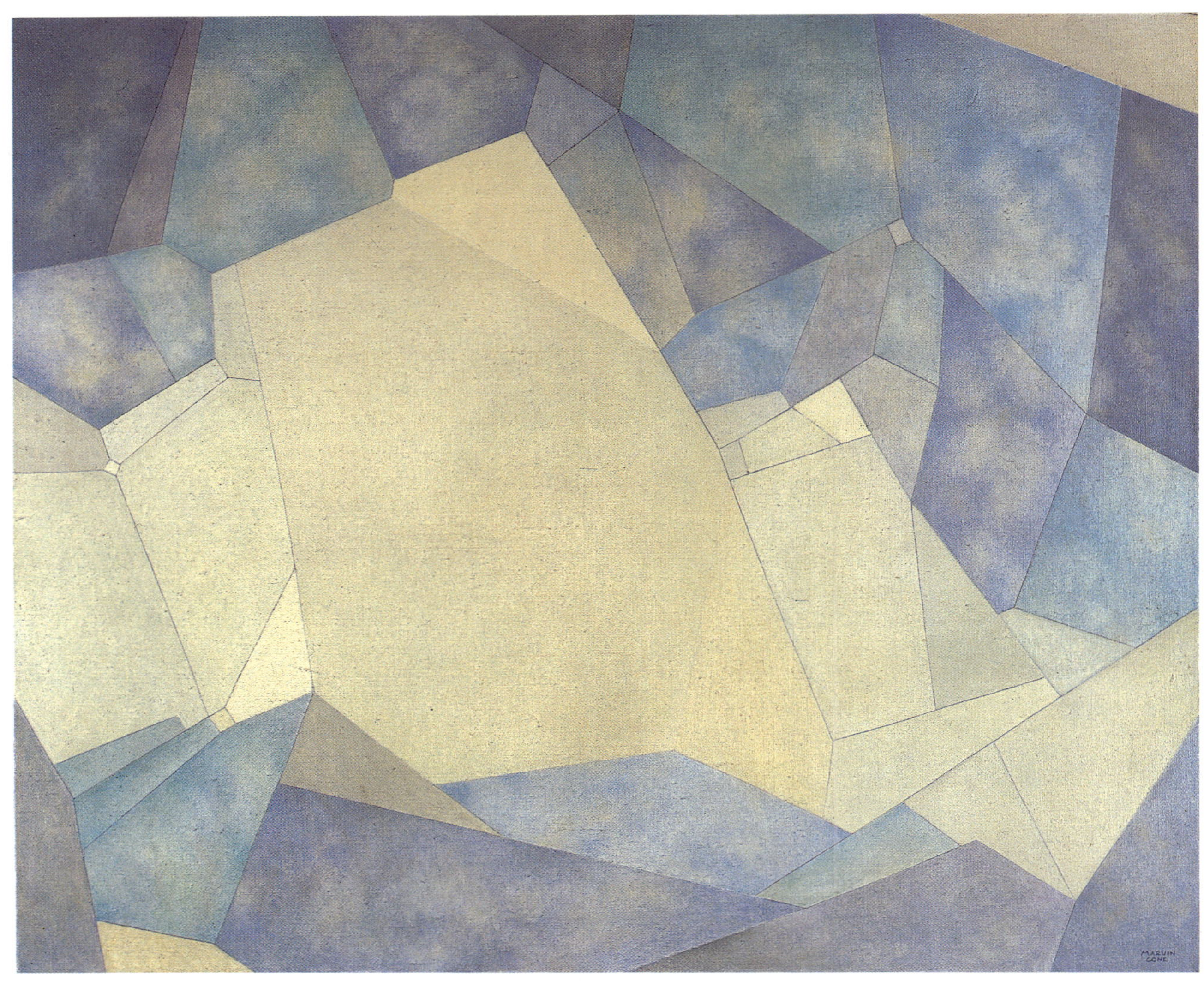


*Blue, Blue-Green, & Yellow No. 1,* 1961. Oil on canvas, 28″ x 34″. (Collection of Winnifred Cone)

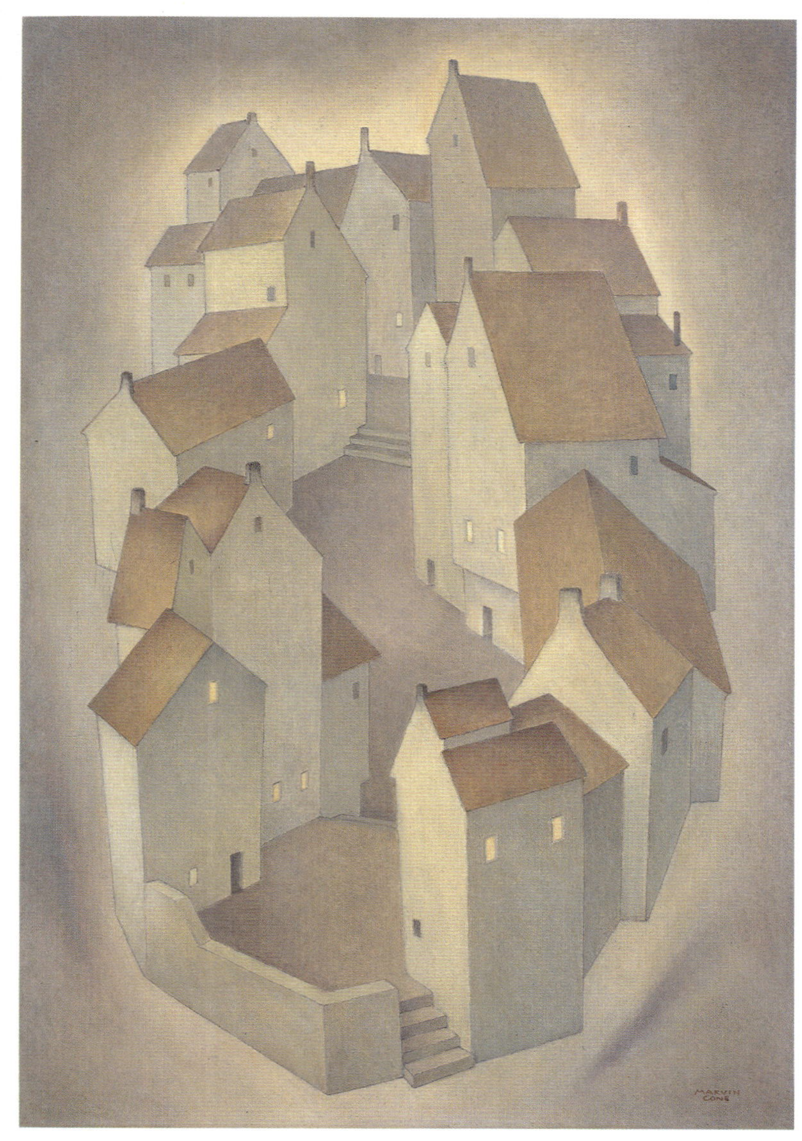


*Christmas Village,* 1961. Oil on canvas, 24¾″ x 16¼″. (Cedar Rapids Museum of Art; Iowa Electric Light & Power Co. Collection)

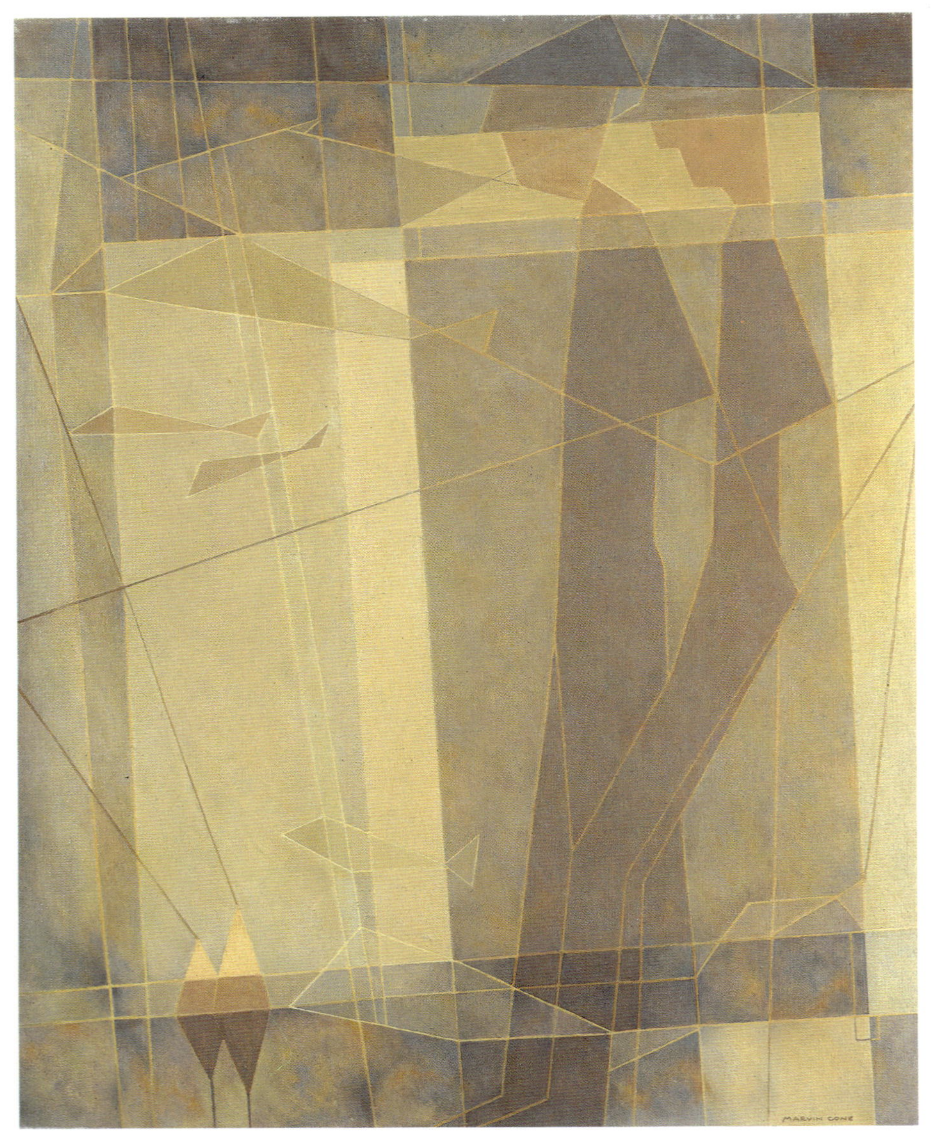


*Fishermen's Dream,* c. 1963. Oil on canvas, 30″ x 23⅞″. (Cedar Rapids Museum of Art; Gift of Winnifred Cone and Family, and Museum Purchase, 1982)

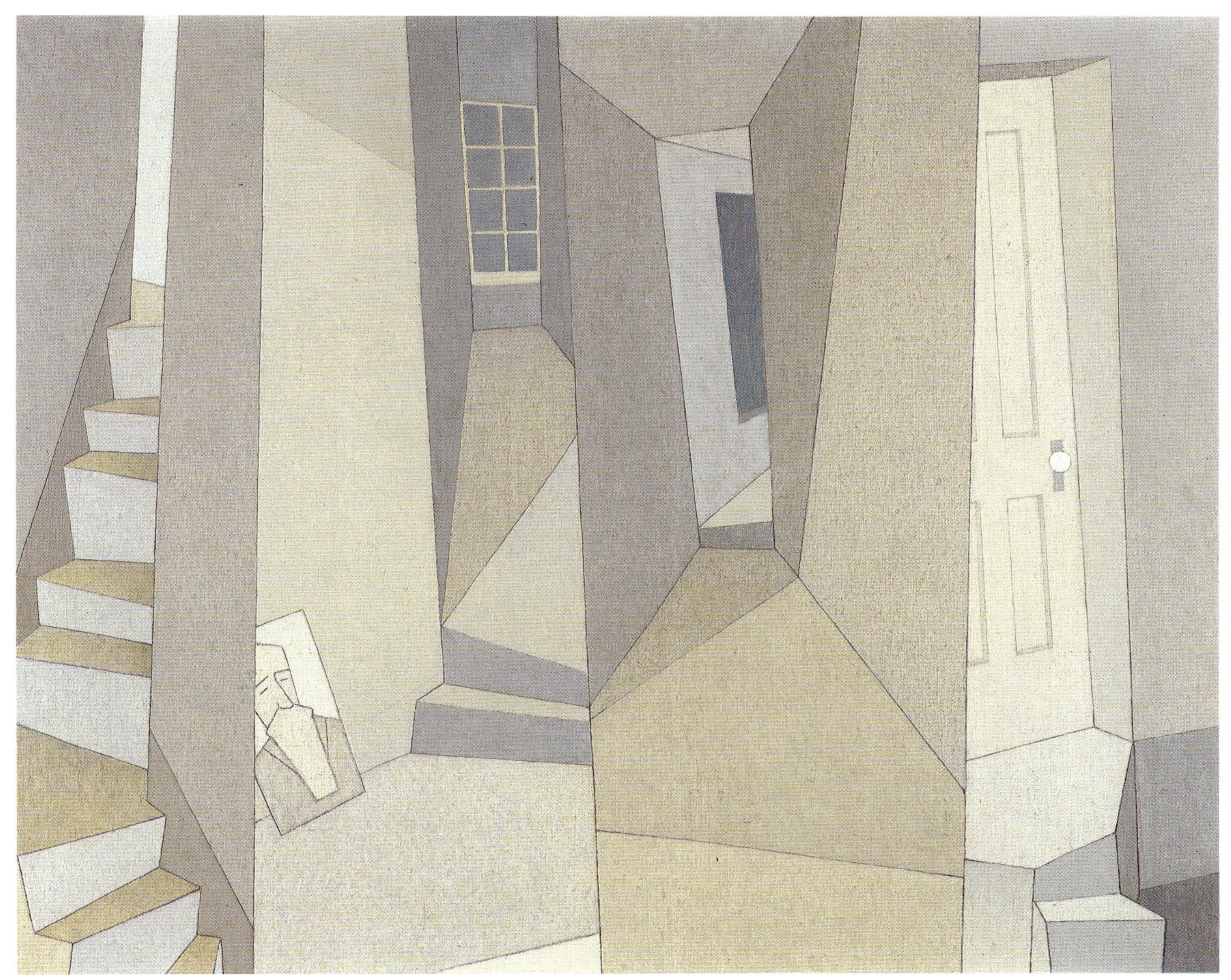

*Four Fragments,* 1964. Oil on canvas, 24″ x 30″. (Collection of Winnifred Cone)